THE GARRETT BLUENOSE PATTERNS

Celebrating Nova Scotia's Rug Hooking Heritage

THE TEACHERS BRANCH,
RUG HOOKING GUILD OF NOVA SCOTIA

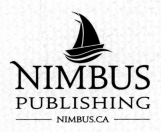

NIMBUS
PUBLISHING
— NIMBUS.CA —

Nimbus Publishing Limited
3660 Strawberry Hill Street,
Halifax, NS, B3K 5A9
(902) 455-4286 nimbus.ca

Printed and bound in China
NB1655

Cover Photos

Top L–R: S-45 Hand-coloured burlap pattern, courtesy of Celia Charlton; S-45 Cottage and sailboat pictorial hooked by Celia Charlton, Bedford, NS.

Second row: John Garrett using a tool to create tiny perforations on paper through which ink was pressed onto burlap. Photo with permission from Anne Sutherland, *The Garrett Family History.*

Third row L–R: Hand-coloured burlap pattern #2024, photo courtesy of Celia Charlton; *Bluenose* ship #2024 hooked by Barbara Surette, Yarmouth, NS, in 2004, photo by Glynis Rogers, courtesy of Leslie Cranley-Blades.

Bottom: Garrett Factory, photo with permission from Anne Sutherland, *The Garrett Family History*.

Back Cover: Cover image of Padulas, 7207 Helen Serrao, Portuguese Cove, NS; 109 Three Bears by Helen Mountain, Lorne, NS, courtesy Betty Oats Calgary, AB; Burlap and Rug hooking tools, courtesy of Paul Downing.

Library and Archives Canada Cataloguing in Publication

Title: The Garrett Bluenose patterns : celebrating Nova Scotia's rug hooking heritage / the Teachers Branch, Rug Hooking Guild of Nova Scotia.
Names: Rug Hooking Guild of Nova Scotia. Teachers Branch, author.
Description: Includes bibliographical references.
Identifiers: Canadiana (print) 20220239460 | Canadiana (ebook) 20220239479 | ISBN 9781774711293 (softcover) | ISBN 9781774711316 (EPUB)
Subjects: LCSH: Bluenose patterns (John E. Garrett Limited) | LCSH: Rugs, Hooked—Nova Scotia—Patterns—History. | LCSH: Rugs, Hooked—Nova Scotia—History.
Classification: LCC TT850 .G37 2022 | DDC 746.7/409716—dc23

Nimbus Publishing acknowledges the financial support for its publishing activities from the Government of Canada, the Canada Council for the Arts, and from the Province of Nova Scotia. We are pleased to work in partnership with the Province of Nova Scotia to develop and promote our creative industries for the benefit of all Nova Scotians.

Dedicated to Linda MacDonald in recognition of her

commitment to the preservation of the Bluenose Patterns

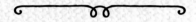

Table of Contents

History of
the Garrett Bluenose Patterns

Arthur and Katherine Garrett's home in Massachusetts with a Bluenose rug in progress.
The pattern, pictured here, is unnumbered but can be found in an old catalogue.
Photo courtesy of the Hooked Rug Museum of North America (HRMNA).

Introduction

The Teachers Branch of the Rug Hooking Guild of Nova Scotia was formed in 1985. It comprises like-minded individuals from around the Maritimes who have formally trained and been certified as rug hooking teachers. Each member brings a unique and valued specialty to the organization.

As outlined in the Code of Ethics, it is the mission of the Teachers Branch to set and maintain a high standard of quality in teaching techniques, craftsmanship, and knowledge of rug hooking; to provide opportunities for study and creative development in all aspects of the craft; to encourage excellence and foster a sense of beauty in colour and design; and to promote the exchange of ideas and information among members of the Guild.

To create and work from a well-designed pattern has always been an exciting part of rug hooking, whether for the teacher, student, or someone who just loves to hook. One always begins with an inspired idea and a vision. The pattern drives our creativity as each loop is pulled.

Garrett was a household name in rug hooking starting in the late nineteenth century, and for over eighty years John Garrett and his son Frank were famous worldwide as important designers of patterns. It is their beautiful and meticulous artistry and attention to detail that took the rug hooking pattern to new levels. Women clamoured for their designs, yarn, and hooks to create beauty, warmth, and colour in their rugs.

Linda MacDonald, one of our Teachers Branch members, acquired the old, forgotten stencil patterns in 1998, left behind after a fire in the Garrett factory in the early 1970s. She bravely resurrected and revived interest in the Garrett Bluenose stencils. At long last, through hard work and ingenuity, she successfully created a number of Bluenose patterns on burlap and linen, making them available to the public again. She had a spirited passion for the heritage of rug hooking and was a strong promoter of the Heritage Rug Registry.

The Teachers Branch is committed to continuing the work that Linda began—the process of preserving the Bluenose patterns for future generations to enjoy. In the following pages you will read the exciting Garrett history and experience what their name stood for—creative excellence in pattern design and production. Suzanne and Hugh Conrod were also dedicated to honouring the past by purchasing Garrett equipment and artifacts for the Hooked Rug Museum of North America (HRMNA) in Hubbards, NS. Suzanne's very kind generosity afforded us, Ruth and Paul Downing, the opportunity to photograph many items featured in this book.

We are truly inspired by the many photos of beautiful Bluenose rugs. Viewing these hooked pieces alongside the old pattern images gives the reader a unique and exciting perspective: history merging with the present. On page after page, one can see that these patterns clearly remain relevant and timeless. Our sincere gratitude is extended to all who took the time to submit photos of their heirloom rugs.

Garrett *Bluenose* pattern 2024: the three stages from paper stencil to burlap pattern to completed 32 x 51-inch (81 x 129.5-cm) hooked rug:

2024 Factory Paper Stencil,
courtesy of Teachers Branch.

2024 Coloured Burlap, Celia Charlton, Bedford, NS.

2024 Hooked by Norma MacLellan, 1981,
courtesy of Ruth Downing.

With sincere appreciation, we gratefully acknowledge the teachers who so kindly volunteered their time and energy to help with the Bluenose project:

- Those who transferred patterns from old factory paper to acetate material: Celia Charlton, Janet Delo, Wanetta Evans, Chris Hay, Jane Holden, Shirley Joyce, Donna Legere, and Anne Lockhart.
- The work party who organized, recorded, and transferred stencils: Chris Hay, Shirley Joyce, Anne Lockhart, and Ruth Downing.
- Those who contributed their comprehensive notes and instructions as a valuable resource.
- The teachers who wrote on a wide range of topics and whose detailed assistance will be of great benefit to rug hookers, regardless of their rug hooking background: Elizabeth Bastin, Celia Charlton, Janet Delo, Dwight Gallagher, Mary Grant, Shirley Joyce, Anne Lockhart, Doris Norman, and Ellen Tancock.
- The compiler and editor of the glossary of terms, Caroline Simpson.

Ruth Downing was given the reins by fellow members of the Teachers Branch to spearhead the Garrett Bluenose project (stencils and book). For over two years Ruth and her husband, Paul, have been dedicated to bringing this enormous challenge to completion. Ruth spent countless hours on the organization, research, and writing. Truly enjoyable was the correspondence with Garrett descendants, Linda MacDonald's husband, Eldon, and all those wonderful rug hookers who so generously shared photos of their work. The Teachers Branch is most grateful to Paul for his support and invaluable technical assistance with the stencil, photo, and book editing. Special thanks to Kevin Downing for the software enhancement of many digital images.

The Garrett Story: A Snapshot

In 1892, John E. Garrett (1865–1937) and his father, Frank, began to design and sell printed burlap patterns out of their home in New Glasgow, NS. John was fascinated by the process and put his artistic talent to great use in the design and creation of patterns. He would later be joined in the business by three sons, Frank, Cecil, and Arthur. Frank was the artist and designer. Cecil managed and coordinated business operations at the New Glasgow plant. Arthur managed the US branch in Malden, Massachusetts. Their business was known as "Garrett's," and their patterns came to be known as "Bluenose" around the year 1926, for the famous Nova Scotia schooner.

Photo with permission from Anne Sutherland, *The Garrett Family History.*

Garrett Factory, photo with permission from Anne Sutherland, *The Garrett Family History.*

(L–R:) Frank, Kate, Arthur (standing), Cecil, and father, John. Photo with permission from Anne Sutherland, Toronto, ON, granddaughter of Cecil Garrett and author of *The Garrett Family History*.

Over the course of eighty years, hundreds of designs were produced by the Garretts. John drew many of the patterns alongside his son Frank, who studied in New York to become a commercial artist in the 1920s. After returning from art school, Frank's immense talent and creative influence brought a fresh look to production. With artistic flair, his designs stood out from the rigid, Victorian-style patterns of the previous years. Popular with rug hookers were florals and scrolls, geometrics, pictorials, animals, and whimsical designs. A number of patterns were a mixture of categories, and many were variations on previous themes.

Rag paper was used for the stencil designs, which were perforated with tiny holes. A machine stamped the designs through the paper onto the burlap with black ink. The burlap was then hand-coloured by factory women to brighten the dull tones of the burlap and to help with colour planning. Jute burlap—made to order in Scotland—was used for its strength. As stated by Suzanne and Hugh Conrod in their book, *Rescued from Oblivion*, "The colourists would be seated on high

John Garrett using a tool to create tiny perforations on paper through which ink was pressed onto burlap. Photo with permission from Anne Sutherland, *The Garrett Family History*.

THE GARRETT BLUENOSE PATTERNS

stools…each of the artists had bottles of varying toned paints before them and they used long handled round brushes to spread on the specified colours in each pattern."

According to the Conrods, "John Garrett was a man with a mission. He sought to create the total package of rug hooking beginning with pattern making to creating the finished product. Ultimately, he had a team of some 30 rug hookers at work creating rugs for sale. He stands in his factory doorway displaying one of his prizes."

Courtesy of HRMNA.

John Garrett, photo courtesy of Suzanne Conrod.

Catalogue image of pattern in Arthur Garrett's home, courtesy of Paul Downing.

Laura Bonnyman, 1866–1907, wife of John Garrett, hooking a Bluenose rug. Photo with permission from Anne Sutherland, *The Garrett Family History*.

Evolution of a Bluenose Rug Pattern

Original pencil sketch by Frank Garrett, 3 x 5 inches. Photo by Paul Downing with permission of HRMNA.

Detailed pencil sketch by Frank Garrett, 1937. Photo by Ruth Downing with permission of HRMNA.

S-45 Original paper factory stencil. Courtesy of Teachers Branch.

S-45 Hand-coloured burlap pattern, courtesy of Celia Charlton.

S-45 Cottage and sailboat pictorial hooked by Celia Charlton, Bedford, NS.

High demand by rug hookers in the early years led to expansion, the use of updated equipment, more advertising through catalogues, and ever-increasing mail-order sales. In the early 1900s, as popularity grew, Eaton's and other department stores began marketing patterns designed for them by the Garrett business. In the late 1920s, Eaton's became their best customer. Garrett's quickly rose to serve all of Canada, the USA, Britain, and eventually the world over as the largest producer of rug hooking patterns.

Throughout the years, many catalogues were produced to advertise patterns and supplies. The first catalogue came out in the late 1880s, and the last one was printed in 1974.

Catalogues from the Garrett family business, photos courtesy of Ruth Downing.

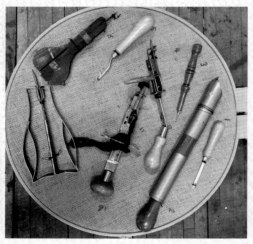

Equipment and rug hooking tools from the Garrett factory on permanent exhibit at HRMNA. (L:) Printer with drum rollers; (C:) Upright lathe for cutting and polishing hooks; (R:) The famous "Rug Hooker" surrounded by a variety of hooks. Photos by Paul Downing, with permission.

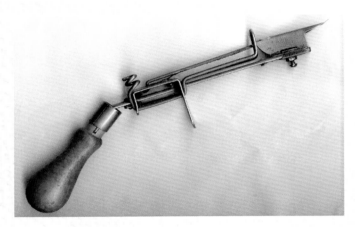

The "Bluenose Hooker," photo with permission from Anne Sutherland, *The Garrett Family History*.

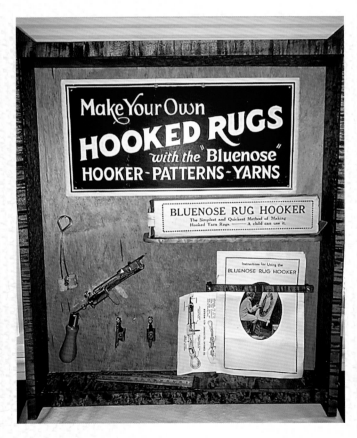

Shadow box of cherished Garrett memorabilia. Courtesy of Nancy MacKenzie, granddaughter of Cecil Garrett, Quispamsis, NB.

Garrett's not only sold patterns, but also wool yarn in a wide variety of colours for hooking. The wool was dyed on-site in six-foot square vats by factory women. Kits were very popular; they included a pattern, yarn, hook, and often a frame. John spent time in the 1920s perfecting a small machine, famously called "Garrett's Rug Hooker" and later, "Little Wonder," specifically designed for hooking with yarn or narrow strips of material. This tool made rug hooking easy and efficient by creating loops of a uniform height. It was so popular that twelve thousand were sold in the first year.

During both world wars, business waned as women turned to other tasks. Also, many supply ships carrying the quality burlap from Scotland were lost at sea during the Second World War. Inferior burlap was not acceptable to the Garretts or their customers. Designing of patterns continued until Frank's death in 1958. Frank's son Cameron took over the business, but by the 1960s, interest in patterns was in deep decline. "Garrett's Bluenose" was renamed "Garrett's-by-the-Bridge" when they began selling antique furniture. Bluenose patterns continued to be sold into the 1980s. A fire at the factory in the early 1970s caused significant water damage and ruined the burlap. The business could not recover financially, and the decision was made to close.

Photo with permission from Anne Sutherland, *The Garrett Family History*.

Advertisement through cardboard signs.
Photo courtesy of Ruth Downing.

Factory yarn sampler, photo courtesy of Diann
MacDonald, Waverley, NS.

The contributions of the Garrett family to the rug hooking world cannot be overstated. For eighty years, they were the largest producer of patterns, selling to thousands of happy customers in many countries. During the past century, their meticulous, beautiful designs have been hooked into colourful finished rugs to grace the walls and floors of homes around the world.

SOURCES

Conrod, Suzanne, and Hugh Conrod. *Rescued from Oblivion: A Hooked Rug Museum of North America Research Project*. Bloomington, Indiana: AuthorHouse, 2010.

Robson, Scott. "Garrett's 'Bluenose' Hooked Rugs," *Before E-Commerce: A History of Canadian Mail-order Catalogues*. Gatineau, Quebec: Canadian Museum of History, 2009. historymuseum.ca/cmc/exhibitions/cpm/catalog/cat2102e.html.

Ryan, Nanette, and Doreen Wright. *Garretts and the Bluenose Rugs of Nova Scotia*. Halifax, NS, 1990.

Sutherland, Anne. "The Garrett Family History: Bluenose Hooked Rug Craft in New Glasgow, NS." Created for her mother, Claire (Garrett) Sutherland, daughter of Cecil Garrett and the family archivist and historian, Toronto, ON, 2013.

The Story Continues
with Linda MacDonald

Linda MacDonald, courtesy of *The Loop* magazine, Issue 40 (3), Summer 2018.

Enter Linda MacDonald, our friend, fellow teacher, and shop owner from Pictou, NS. She saw an opportunity to rescue the stencils from the basement of the factory to protect and preserve them for future generations of rug hookers. In the spring of 1998, Linda approached Cameron Garrett and former manager Eddie MacArthur to purchase the stencils and old burlap patterns. We are able to picture Linda, small but mighty, tramping through the dirt and grime of the basement in her rubber boots on a mission to recover as many stencils as possible.

Linda sorted and labelled over three hundred designs. She transferred many patterns from the old factory paper to acetate material, which is an archival-quality, medium-weight, clear transparency. The Garretts did not number their patterns in sequence, and accurate records do not exist for the dating of their patterns. For almost twenty years, Linda dedicated herself to promoting the heritage of the Bluenose designs and successfully created and sold their patterns through her business, Rags to Rugs.

Sadly, Linda passed away suddenly in May 2018. She is greatly missed, and her loss has been deeply felt in the rug hooking community. She touched everyone with her talent, commitment, and dedication. She was a fine teacher and mentor, introducing many to the art of rug hooking through classes and workshops. A hard-working individual, she was very active with the Rug Hooking Guild of Nova Scotia as past president and earned our respect as a truly wonderful Rug School director.

A great believer in honouring the past, Linda passionately promoted the heritage mat. We owe her a debt of gratitude for her dedication and great foresight in preserving the Garrett Bluenose patterns.

Bluenose Rug 15, hooked by Linda MacDonald, Pictou, NS, courtesy of Dwight Gallagher.

The Ship *Hector*, a 2003 featured pattern, hooked by Linda MacDonald, Pictou, NS, courtesy of Eldon MacDonald.

This pattern was made available to the public by Linda for the 230th anniversary of the landing of the *Hector*. To quote Linda, "In September 1773 the ship *Hector* arrived in Pictou, NS, with approximately two hundred settlers from the Scottish Highlands. This landing is celebrated as the beginning of Scottish settlement in Nova Scotia. The *Hector* pattern was first printed by the Garretts in 1923 to commemorate the 150th anniversary of the landing."

The Teachers Branch Becomes Involved

In October 2019, at the invitation of the Teachers Branch of the Rug Hooking Guild of Nova Scotia, 120 rug hookers came together in Pictou, NS, for a workshop event to remember Linda and celebrate her passion for heritage rugs. A selection of four Bluenose chair mat patterns—925 Cottage Scene, 957 Floral, 977 Leaves, and 940 *Bluenose* Ship—were hooked by attendees, with instruction provided by teachers. It was a great day for all participants. Their submissions are featured in the "Chair Mats" section of this book.

In November 2019, the Teachers Branch was approached by Linda's husband, Eldon, to purchase the original factory paper stencils and acetate. Appreciating the historical value, our members enthusiastically agreed to take on the project, knowing we could properly care for the stencils. In December, Ruth and Paul Downing moved two truckloads of stencils from Pictou to their garage in Cow Bay, NS.

Collecting paper and acetate stencils from
Eldon MacDonald, Pictou, NS.

Preparing original paper factory stencils for
copying onto acetate.

THE GARRETT BLUENOSE PATTERNS

Bluenose paper stencils prepared for archival storage.

An important find; we could "bear-ly" believe our luck! Number 117, Frank Garrett's whimsical design, and a bestseller of the Garrett patterns.

A number of the paper stencils were too old to salvage. They had become brittle over time and crumbled like dry leaves. Having been subjected to a fire and two floods did not help. However, many did survive. During the winter of 2020, Ruth and Paul spent several weeks cleaning and categorizing four hundred stencils. It was gritty work with masks and gloves, requiring great care in handling the old paper. The survivors were rolled into tubes, relabelled, catalogued, and placed in plastic totes to await archival storage at a museum.

After the cleanup, Ruth put aside over one hundred paper stencils for Teachers Branch members to later transfer onto acetate. The plan was to substantially add to the collection started by Linda.

During the spring and summer of 2020, eight teachers very kindly volunteered their time to transfer the old factory stencils to acetate. In November, 220 acetate stencils were painstakingly scanned by the Dartmouth, NS, print shop, Cansel, to create PDF files. Because

Transferring from coloured burlap onto acetate material; Chris Hay and Shirley Joyce with the Bluenose 3005 Bucking Bronco, designed by Miller Tibbetts. Photos by Ruth Downing.

of the poor condition of many factory stencils, some of the images were scanned from various old Garrett catalogues in order to preserve them for the future. Teachers Branch members unanimously decided that the PDFs of the patterns should be made available to all members of the Rug Hooking Guild of Nova Scotia at a minimal cost through the RHGNS website (rhgns.com). These PDFs and the scanned catalogue images were uploaded to the Guild website on July 1, 2021, the launch date.

The Teachers Branch is dedicated to the preservation and promotion of the historically important Garrett Bluenose patterns. With a treasure trove of over 240 beautiful and timeless designs, we honour this rich and vast part of our rug hooking heritage. This has been an exciting chapter in our lives and a labour of love as we've worked with the old factory paper stencils to create patterns to be preserved for generations to come.

Linda MacDonald's acetates.

Teachers Branch's newly completed acetate rolls.

The Hooked Rug Museum of North America

Suzanne and Hugh Conrod founded the Hooked Rug Museum of North America (HRMNA). They acquired the building in Hubbards, NS, in 2009, and the museum officially opened in June 2013. Its extensive collection of hand-hooked rugs and artifacts preserves the important heritage and future development of this fibre art. Suzanne is the founding director, chair, and art liaison for the museum.

In 2004, with the development of a museum in mind, Suzanne and Hugh explored the Garrett factory basement in New Glasgow, NS, in hopes of acquiring equipment and memorabilia. They had the help of Eddie McArthur, the former manager of the Garrett factory and owner of Garrett's-by-the-Bridge. After a number of trips to the grisly interior of the fire- and water-damaged basement to recover and purchase what they could, they made important and astounding finds. One was a box of original pencil sketches and pen-and-ink drawings for the Bluenose patterns, all postcard-sized and smaller. These tiny, meticulous designs would have been drawn by John and Frank. In their book, *Rescued from Oblivion*, Suzanne and Hugh said of their discovery, "Seemingly reluctant, the box gradually disclosed its real treasure. Slowly unveiled to us were stacks of loosely assembled original pen and ink sketches…each delicately drawn image was little more than 4 x 6 inches in size, sometimes smaller…. We were celebrating an exquisite treasure…. More than

834 Floral pen-and-ink drawing, courtesy of HRMNA.

300 immaculate images from yesteryear were rug hooking history's reward that day. The past was speaking to us through the creativity of two early Canadian rug designers, John and Frank Garrett."

In February 2021, we (Ruth and Paul Downing) approached Sherry Chandler, a co-director of the HRMNA, with a request to photograph the Garrett machinery and artifacts that are on permanent exhibit. Suzanne and Sherry very graciously opened the doors of the museum and gave us access to the Garrett room and memorabilia on display. With the permission of the museum, we took photographs to capture for the reader a bygone era in rug hooking pattern production. Most special in our findings, and forever etched in our memories, was the box filled with the original pen-and-ink drawings, which are not on view to the public. We photographed a number of the pencil sketches and ink drawings that are featured in these pages. As we briefly took a step back in time, we were able to imagine father and son working on each meticulous drawing, all amazingly detailed pieces of art.

The rug hooking world recognizes the importance of the contributions and the enormous time and effort invested by the Conrods and their research team in order to preserve this nearly forgotten part of our rug hooking heritage. Ever since its opening, the Hooked Rug Museum of North America has welcomed thousands through its halls to view and admire the past and the present.

7118 Geometric catalogue image, courtesy of Teachers Branch.

Bluenose Hooked Rugs: A Celebration of Old and New

S-45 Coloured burlap and hooked rug with wool and yarn. Arrangement by Celia Charlton, Bedford, NS.

Welcome Mats

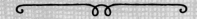

HR-20 Welcome mat pen-and-ink drawing, courtesy of HRMNA.

HR-38 Mary Grant, Fredericton, NB.

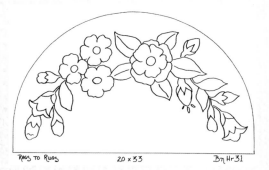

HR-31 Acetate, courtesy of Teachers Branch.

HR-31 Tanya McNutt, Truro, NS.

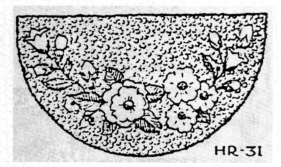

HR-31 Catalogue image.

HR-31 Shirley Bradshaw, Yarmouth, NS.

HR-31 Adaptation, Jean Chipman, Berwick, NS.

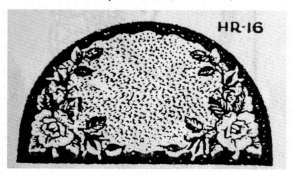

HR-16 Catalogue, courtesy of Teachers Branch.

THE GARRETT BLUENOSE PATTERNS

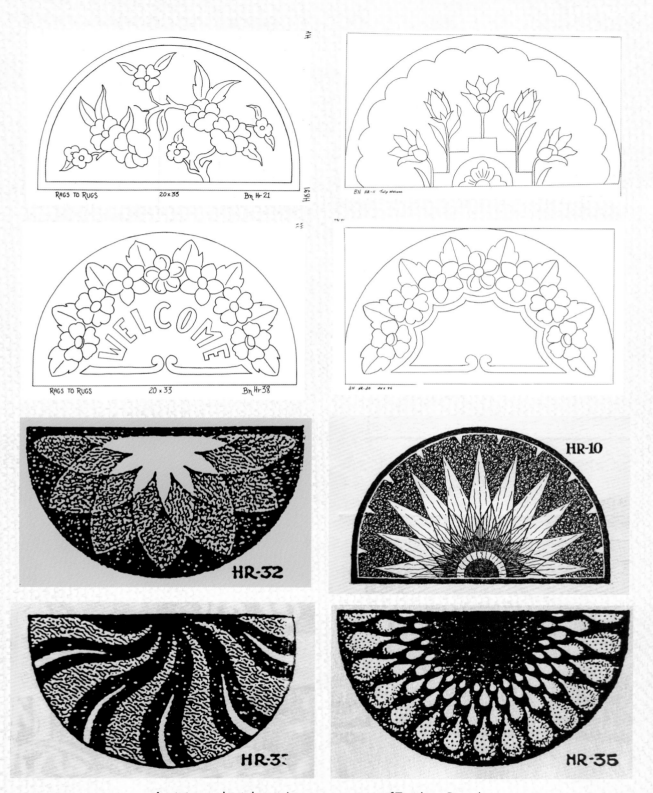

Acetates and catalogue images, courtesy of Teachers Branch.

Chair Mats

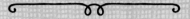

946 Original pen-and-ink drawing, courtesy of HRMNA.

925 Cottage Scenes, Workshop for Linda MacDonald

Original ink drawing, 3 x 3 inches, courtesy of HRMNA.

Carrie Byers, courtesy of Judy Langille, Truro, NS.

Chris Hay, Dartmouth, NS.

Jean Purdy, Bible Hill, NS.

Judy Langille, Truro, NS.

925 Acetate, courtesy of Teachers Branch.

Dwight Gallagher, Springhill, NS.

Judy Langille, Truro, NS.

Karen Cross, Dartmouth, NS.

Ruth Downing, Cow Bay, NS.

Ruby MacKenzie, Scotsburn, NS.

957 Floral Hexagons, Workshop for Linda MacDonald

Original ink drawing, Frank Garrett,
courtesy of HRMNA.

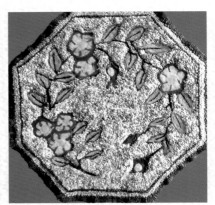  

(L:) Donna Legere, Nappan, NS; (C:) Patricia McLelland, Dartmouth, NS;
(R:) Caroll Anne MacDonald, Dartmouth, NS.

(L:) Caroline Simpson, Fredericton, NB; (C:) Gloria Young, Bible Hill, NS;
(R:) Jane Holden, Halifax NS.

THE GARRETT BLUENOSE PATTERNS

940 *Bluenose* Schooner, Workshop for Linda MacDonald

940 *Bluenose* chair mats, original pencil sketch, Frank Garrett, courtesy of HRMNA.

Jeanne Purdy, Bible Hill, NS.

Anne Lockhart, Millvale, PE.

Ellen Tancock, Canning, NS.

Doris Norman, Fredericton, NB.

940 *Bluenose* Schooner

(L:) 940 Acetate, Teachers Branch; (C:) Martha Morgan, 1960s, Central Caribou, NS;
(R:) Tracy Holmes, Nine Mile Creek, PE.

(L): Catalogue image, Teachers Branch; (C:) Celia Charlton, Bedford, NS;
(R:) Elizabeth Bastin, Fredericton, NB.

940 *Bluenose* chair mats, Linda MacDonald, Pictou, NS.

THE GARRETT BLUENOSE PATTERNS

977 Maple Leaves, Workshop for Linda MacDonald

Acetate, courtesy of Teachers Branch.

Linda MacDonald, Pictou, NS.

Ruby MacKenzie, Scotsburn, NS.

977 Three variations: embroidery punch, Oxford punch and hooked, Donna Legere, Nappan, NS.

Leslie Cranley-Blades, Yarmouth, NS.

Mary Grant, Fredericton, NB.

Shirley Joyce, Pictou, NS.

Floral Chair Mats

946 Daisy, acetate,
Teachers Branch.

Shirley Joyce, Pictou, NS.

Acetates and catalogue images, courtesy of Teachers Branch.

Geometric Chair Mats

945 Pinwheel acetate,
Teachers Branch.

Elizabeth Bastin, Fredericton, NB

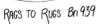

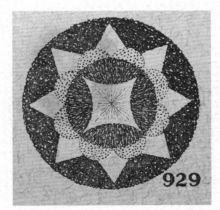

Acetates and catalogue images, courtesy of Teachers Branch.

Pictorials

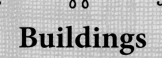

Buildings

Pencil sketch, Frank Garrett, 1937, courtesy of HRMNA.

872 Farm Scene

Original pen-and-ink drawing, HRMNA.

872 Farm scene, Ruby MacKenzie, Scotsburn, NS, 2019.

872 Acetate, courtesy of Teachers Branch.

3027 Homestead, acetate, courtesy of Teachers Branch.

3027 Homestead, Suzanne Leroux.

133 Homestead, Barbara Surette, Yarmouth, NS, 2000,
courtesy of Leslie Cranley-Blades.

Original pen-and-ink sketch, HRMNA.

874 Marie Marple, Calgary, AB, 2017.

874 Diann MacDonald, Waverley, NS.

874 Helen Mountain, Lorne, NS,
courtesy of Betty Oates.

874 Celia Charlton, Bedford, NS.

874 Helen Mountain, Lorne, NS,
courtesy of Betty Oates.

S-50 Hunter's Cabin

Original pencil sketch, 3 x 5 inches, HRMNA.

Factory stencil 28 x 48, Courtesy of Teachers Branch

S-50 Shirley Joyce, Pictou, NS.

S-50 Helen Rufelds, Fredericton, NB.

S-46 House by the Water

S-46 House by the Water, acetate, Teachers Branch.

S-46 House by the Water, Velma Black, Calgary, AB, 2007,
courtesy of Marie Marple.

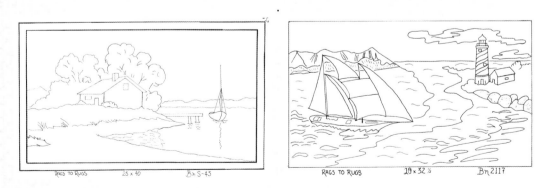

Acetates, courtesy of Teachers Branch.

THE GARRETT BLUENOSE PATTERNS

S-45 Pencil sketch by Frank Garrett, 1937, HRMNA.

S-721 Sketch by Frank Garrett, HRMNA.

S-45 Celia Charlton, Bedford, NS.

S-721 Tracy Holmes, Nine Mile Creek. PE.

753 English Cottage, original pen-and-ink, HRMNA.

53 English cottage, coloured burlap, courtesy of
Celia Charlton, Bedford, NS.

12 Coloured burlap, courtesy of Celia Charlton, Bedford, NS.

Pictorials

Bluenose Schooners

Original pencil sketch by Frank Garrett, 1920s, courtesy of HRMNA.

Pencil sketch by Frank Garrett, 1920s.

304 Pen-and-ink drawing variation, courtesy of HRMNA.

2024 Factory paper stencil, courtesy of Teachers Branch.

(L:) 2024 Coloured burlap, Celia Charlton, Bedford, NS;
(R:) 2024 Helen Mountain, Lorne, NS, 1960s, courtesy of Betty Oates.

THE GARRETT BLUENOSE PATTERNS

2024 Coloured burlap, Shirley Bradshaw, Yarmouth, NS.

2024 Doris Norman, Fredericton, NB, 1988.

B-100 Coloured burlap.

B-100 Rug, Leslie Langille, Clementsport, NS.

(L:) 2024 Coloured burlap, Leslie Langille, Clementsport, NS, courtesy of Ellen Tancock;
(R:) 2024 Barbara Surette, Yarmouth, NS, 2004, photo by Glynis Rogers, courtesy of Leslie Cranley-Blades.

2002 Spanish Galleon; 2011 Clipper Ship; 304 *Bluenose*; original pen-and-inks, courtesy of HRMNA.

Images from Bluenose catalogues, courtesy of Teachers Branch.

Animals

2009 Moose, original pen-and-ink, 3 x 5 inches, courtesy of HRMNA.

Garrett Factory staffer showing use of Bluenose rug hooker tool, courtesy of HRMNA.

2112 Rooster, Shirley Bradshaw, Yarmouth, NS.

2112 Rooster, acetate, courtesy of Teachers Branch.

40 Horned Owl, catalogue image.

Acetate, Teachers Branch.

THE GARRETT BLUENOSE PATTERNS

(L:) 760 Bird on coloured burlap, Betty Callaghan, PE;
(R:) 881 Flying Ducks, coloured burlap, Celia Charlton, Bedford, NS.

Two Swans, Four Variations

O-2 Original reversed stencil.

186 Eaton's pattern,
Caroline Simpson, Fredericton, NB.

829 Swans and 829C Swans with Flowers, courtesy of Teachers Branch.

418 Three Geese, Linda MacDonald, Pictou, NS, courtesy of Dwight Gallagher.

657 Scottie

657 Pencil sketch, HRMNA.

657 Original ink drawing, HRMNA.

657 Scottie, original ink drawing, HRMNA.

(L:) 657 Scottie, coloured burlap, Shirley Bradshaw, Yarmouth, NS;
(R:) 657 Scottie, coloured burlap, Caroline Simpson, Fredericton, NB.

657 Scottie, Celia Charlton, Bedford, NS.

Other Canine Friends

Wooden template from 1800s, HRMNA.

(L:) 2007 Collie, original pen-and-ink drawing, HRMNA;
(R:) 22 (also 2007) Collie, hand-coloured burlap, courtesy of HRMNA.

 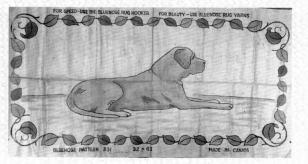

(L:) 831 Catalogue, Teachers Branch; (R:) 831 Coloured burlap, Celia Charlton, Bedford, NS.

NF Catalogue image, courtesy of Teachers Branch.

Two Cats

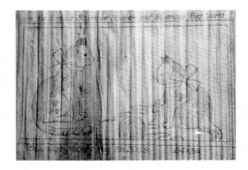

2059 Two Cats, paper stencil, courtesy of Teachers Branch.

(L:) 2059 Two Cats, acetate, courtesy of Teachers Branch;
(R:) 44 Basket of Kittens, Clara Bell Hartling, Kentville, NS, courtesy of Leslie Cranley-Blades.

2059 Two Cats, Anne and Jean Watson, Dartmouth, NS.

2059 Two Cats, Helen Mountain, Lorne, NS, courtesy of Betty Oates.

Stag

(L:) 2055 Stag Head, original pencil sketch, HRMNA;
(R:) 2055 Stag Head, original pen-and-ink drawing, HRMNA.

 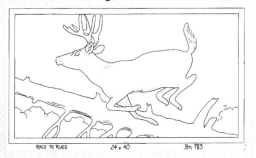

(L:) 783 Jumping Stag, designed by Miller Tibbetts, original pen-and-ink, HRMNA;
(R:) 783 Jumping Stag, acetate, courtesy of Teachers Branch.

783 Jan Lord-Giraldi, Guelph, Ontario.   Elizabeth Jane Maddison, Springhill, NS.

Emily Gallagher, 1960s, Mapleton, NS, courtesy of Dwight Gallagher.

2009 Moose

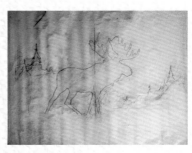 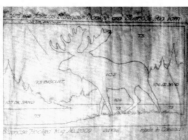 

(L:) Factory stencil, courtesy of Teachers Branch;
(C:) Factory stencil, courtesy of Teachers Branch;
(R:) 2009 Coloured burlap, courtesy of Winnie Glavine, Paradise, NL.

2009 Barbara Surette, Yarmouth, NS,
courtesy of Leslie Cranley-Blades.

2009 Shirley Joyce, Pictou, NS.

Beaver

770 Beavers, coloured burlap,
Caroline Simpson, Fredericton, NB.

770 Beavers, Helen Mountain, Lorne, NS,
courtesy of Betty Oates.

Whimsical Designs

752 Mother Duck, original pen-and-ink, courtesy of HRMNA.

637 Dancing Rabbits, hooked by Iris Richards, Yarmouth, NS.
Photo by Frieda Perry, courtesy of Leslie Cranley-Blades.

Iris Richards, 98, with her rug at the Yarmouth County Museum's rug display
for the fortieth anniversary of the Rug Hooking Guild of Nova Scotia. Photo
by Frieda Perry, courtesy of Leslie Cranley-Blades.

637 and 7115 Catalogue images, courtesy of Teachers Branch.

7123, 7124, and 656 Catalogue images, courtesy of Teachers Branch.

D-4 Two Scotties, Elizabeth Jane Maddison, Springhill, NS, courtesy of Dwight Gallagher.

Three Bears 109, 117–
Among the most popular of the Garrett designs

117 and 109 Three Bears, original pen-and-ink drawing, courtesy of HRMNA.

109 Muriel Stevens, courtesy of Kathryn Hanson, Saint John, NB.

109 Helen Mountain, Lorne, NS,
courtesy of Betty Oates, Calgary, AB.

THE GARRETT BLUENOSE PATTERNS

117 Paper stencil, courtesy of Teachers Branch.

117 Coloured burlap, courtesy of Caroline Simpson, Fredericton, NB.

117 Elizabeth Jane Maddison, Springhill, NS.
Courtesy of Dwight Gallagher.

2015 Three Pigs, Shirley Bradshaw, Yarmouth, NS.

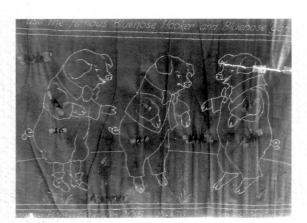

2015 Three Pigs, courtesy of Teachers Branch..

2069 Two Ducklings, Helen Mountain, Lorne, NS,
courtesy of Betty Oates, Calgary, AB.

Geometrics

563 Cosmo, original ink drawing, courtesy of HRMNA.

7238 Deco Flowers, geometric, courtesy of HRMNA.

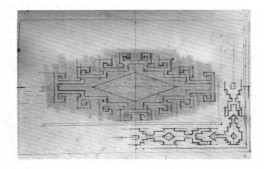 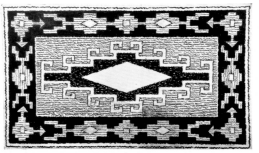

(L:) 112 Geometric, original partial pencil sketch, HRMNA;
(R:) 112 Original pen-and-ink drawing, HRMNA.

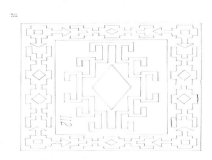

112 Geometric, acetate, courtesy of Teachers Branch.

 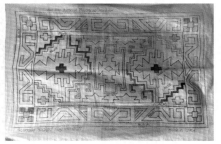

(L:) 4011 Original pen-and-ink drawing, HRMNA;
(R:) 4011 Geometric, coloured burlap, courtesy of HRMNA.

4011 Geometric, acetate, courtesy of Teachers Branch.

THE GARRETT BLUENOSE PATTERNS

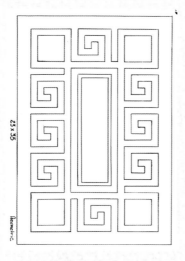

122 Greek Key, acetate,
Teachers Branch.

122 Doris Norman,
Fredericton, NB, 2020.

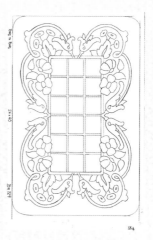

729 Paper stencil,
Teachers Branch.

729 Shirley Good.

Acetate, Teachers Branch.

729 Floral and geometric, Linda Willey.

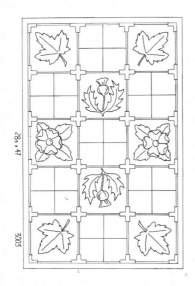

(L:) 3003 Rose and Thistle, acetate, courtesy of Teachers Branch;
(R:) 3003 Rose and Thistle, Elizabeth Bastin, Fredericton, NB.

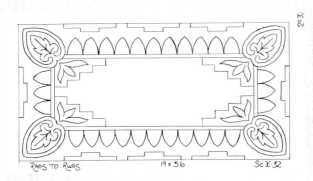

SCX 32 Acetate, courtesy of Teachers Branch.

SCX 32 Ruby MacKenzie, Scotsburn, NS.

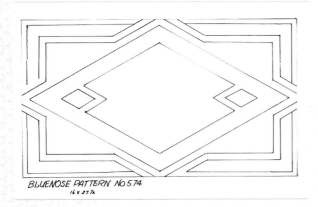
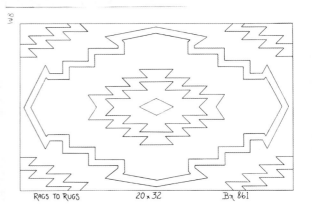

574 Acetate, courtesy of Teachers Branch.

861 Acetate, courtesy of Teachers Branch.

THE GARRETT BLUENOSE PATTERNS

(L:) 7230 Image from catalogue, Teachers Branch;
(R:) 7230 Tessie Hiltz, courtesy of Kathryn Hanson.

O-27 and O-25 Catalogue images, courtesy of Teachers Branch.

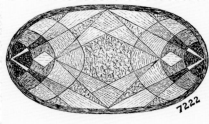

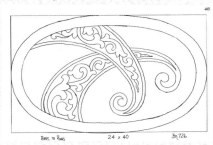

7222 Catalogue image and 726 acetate, courtesy of Teachers Branch.

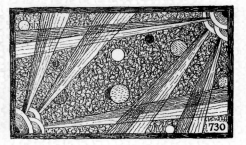

7118 and 730 Catalogue images, courtesy of Teachers Branch.

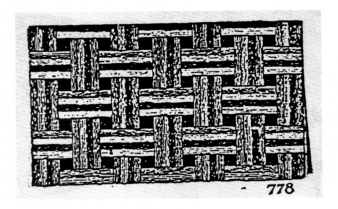

778 Catalogue image , courtesy Teachers Branch.

778 Basket weave, Jean Chipman,
Dartmouth and Berwick, NS, courtesy of Ellen Tancock.

883 Inch mat, Jean Chipman, Dartmouth, Berwick, NS, 2001,
courtesy of Ellen Tancock.

THE GARRETT BLUENOSE PATTERNS

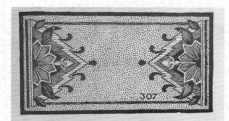

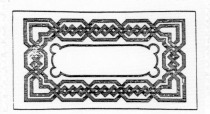

789 Original pen-and-ink drawing, HRMNA.
Catalogue images, courtesy of Teachers Branch.

1054 Catalogue image, Teachers Branch.

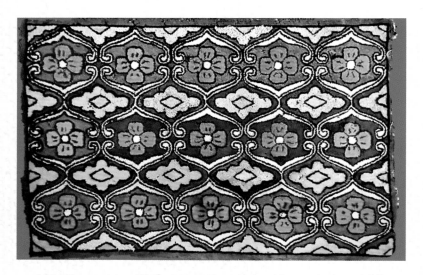

1054 Geometric with flower centres, Helen Mountain, Lorne, NS,
courtesy of Betty Oates, Calgary, AB.

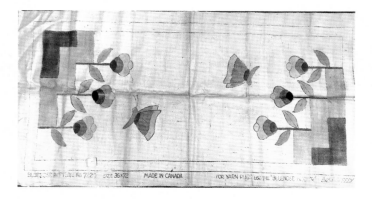

7220 Coloured burlap, courtesy of Celia Charlton, Bedford, NS.

Florals and Scrolls

NF Original pen-and-ink drawing, courtesy of HRMNA.

1002 Original pen-and-ink drawing, courtesy of HRMNA.

805 Basket of flowers, coloured burlap and finished rug, with permission, HRMNA.

805 Acetate, courtesy of Teachers Branch.

805 Louise Corbett, Halifax, NS.

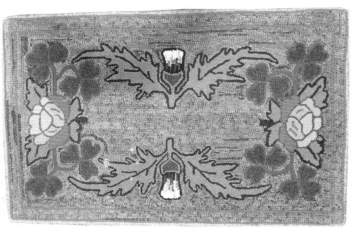

546 Original pen-and-ink drawing, HRMNA.

546 Celia Charlton, Bedford, NS.

THE GARRETT BLUENOSE PATTERNS

11 Acetate, courtesy of Teachers Branch.

11 Oval roses, Judy Langille, Truro, NS.

125 Clara Hartling, Kentville, NS, courtesy of Leslie Cranley-Blades.

282 Ralph's roses, acetate, Teachers Branch.

282 Shirley Joyce, Pictou, NS.

O-52 Oval roses, Charlotte Fraser.

213 Wild roses, Jean Chipman, Berwick, NS,
courtesy of Ellen Tancock.

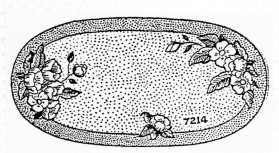

7214 Image from catalogue.

7214, James Henry Louis, 1960s, Juniper, NB,
courtesy of Lil Gruntz.

THE GARRETT BLUENOSE PATTERNS

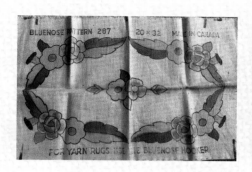

287 Coloured burlap and finished rug, Carol Bryson, Halifax, NS.

130 and 287 Coloured burlaps, courtesy of Shirley Bradshaw, Yarmouth, NS.

315 Eaton's, coloured pattern, Edith Whynot, Bridgewater, NS, courtesy of Helen MacMillan.

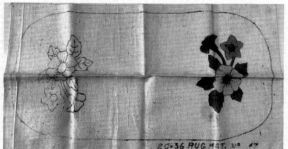

2103 and 47 Roses on coloured burlap, Leslie Langille, Clementsport, NS.

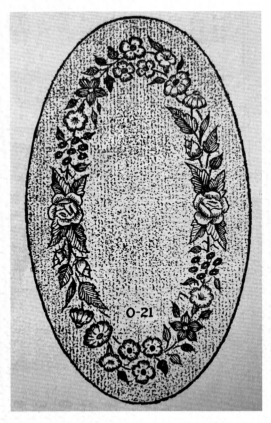

O-21, Image from catalogue.

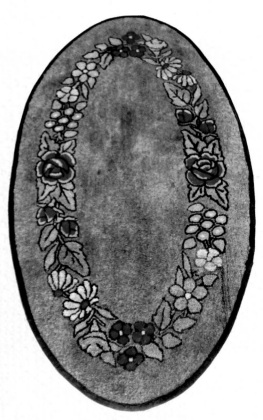

O-21 Sue Ellen Askeland (Robertson), Stellarton, NS.

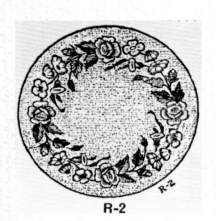

R-2 and 4000 Catalogue images, courtesy of Teachers Branch.

2109 Paper stencil, courtesy of Teachers Branch.

2109 Acetate, courtesy of Teachers Branch.

2109 Audrey Norman, St. Andrews, NB.

9250 Piano bench, Marie Marple, Calgary, AB.

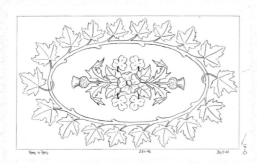

O-41 Acetate, Teachers Branch.

O-41 Gayle Wynn, Truro, NS.

803 Elizabeth Jane Maddison, Springhill, NS.　　603 Elizabeth Jane Maddison, Springhill, NS.

775 Twigs and leaves, Tanya McNutt, Truro, NS.　　775 Lynda Stevenson, Masstown, NS.

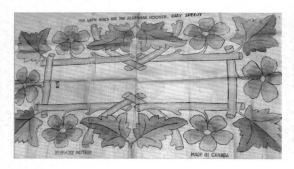

630 Coloured burlap and finished rug, Betty Callaghan, PE.

559 Betty Callaghan, PE.　　3002 Helen Mountain, Lorne, NS,
courtesy of Betty Oates.

873 Colchester Heritage Rug Hookers, hospital auxiliary mat, Truro, NS, courtesy of Ursula Gulliver.

873 Celia Charlton, Bedford, NS.

873 Celia Charlton, courtesy of her Grand-dog, Waffles. Bluenose Rugs underfoot!

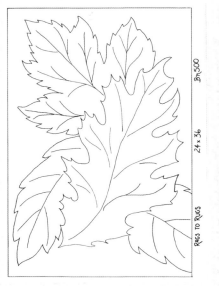 

500 Acetate, Teachers Branch. 500 Ruby MacKenzie, Scotsburn, NS.

(L:) 2103 Coloured burlap, Celia Charlton, Bedford, NS;
(R:) 297 Coloured burlap, Celia Charlton, Bedford, NS.

(L:) 161 Edith Whynot, Bridgewater, NS, courtesy of Helen McMillan;
(R:) Coloured burlap, Celia Charlton, Bedford, NS.

THE GARRETT BLUENOSE PATTERNS

7207 Pen-and-ink drawing, HRMNA.

7207 Helen Serrao, Portuguese Cove, NS.

Acetate, Teachers Branch.

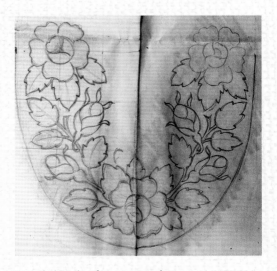

Pencil sketch of roses, Frank Garrett, HRMNA.

Mixed Category

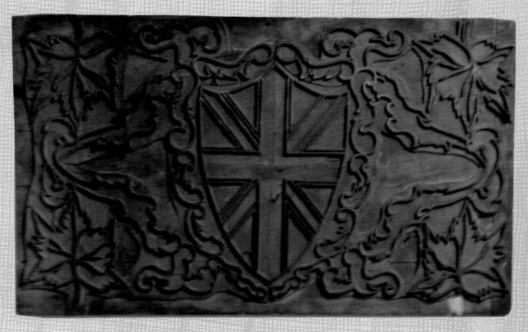

Pre-1892 Union Jack shield, hand-carved wood pattern, courtesy of HRMNA.

Mixed Category

NF Bluenose pattern, Teachers Branch.

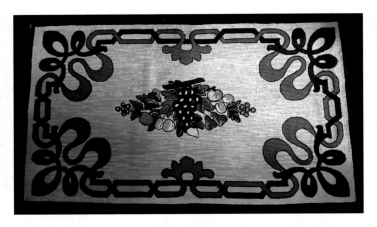

NF Helen Mountain, Lorne, NS, courtesy of Betty Oates.

2087 Paper stencil,
courtesy of Teachers Branch.

2087 Tree of life, Doris Norman,
Fredericton, NB.

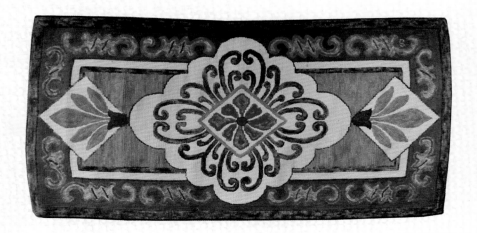

4009 Helen Serrao, Portuguese Cove, NS.

4009 Acetate, courtesy of Teachers Branch.

790 Good luck, paper stencil,
Teachers Branch.

790 Beverly Levine, Truro, NS.

800 Original pen-and-ink, courtesy of HRMNA.

800 Elizabeth Bastin, Fredericton, NB.

NF Shirley Joyce, Pictou, NS.

Teachers Branch:
Notes and Instructions

2041 Original pen-and-ink drawing, courtesy of HRMNA.

Rug Hooking: A Beginner's Guide

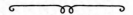

Ellen Tancock

So, you want to be a rug hooker! Maybe you have a dear sweet mother or grandmother who works tirelessly on their beautiful rugs, and you want to share this craft with them. Or you may have heard of rug hooking or have seen some gorgeous rugs that people have created so you've decided to give it a try. Well, it's easy, so let's start. I guarantee you will get hooked!

As a beginning rug hooker, you may have many questions regarding this amazing craft and beautiful art form. The humble beginnings of rug hooking date back many years to simple homes where, using leftover clothes and feed bags, rugs were made for the floors. Rug hooking is part of our heritage and continues to draw people; it elicits wonder in both those admiring and those creating these beautiful rugs.

What supplies and tools do I need to hook?

- Backing material such as linen, monks cloth, rug warp, or burlap. The type of backing material you select depends on whether you are doing a wall hanging, a table mat, or a floor rug. To be ready to hook, have your pattern drawn on your backing or purchase a backing with the pattern already on it.

- A frame or hoop specifically for rug hooking. It is helpful to try using one before purchasing your frame.

- Lots of beautiful wool cut into wool strips. A size #5 or #6 cut is a good size to learn to rug hook, because the width of the wool strip is easy to handle. Traditional rug hooking uses 100 percent wool fabric, and the wool strips must be cut absolutely straight or they will fall apart.

- A hook with the tip and shank sized for the #5 or #6 cut wool; choose a hook that is comfortable in your hand. There are many types of hooks available, from fine to coarse, depending on what size cut wool you are using.

- Small scissors that are sharp, straight or bent, and able to cut through wool fabric.

- A Sharpie fine-tipped marker.

How much wool do I need?

- One way to figure out approximately how much wool you need is to take a piece of wool fabric, fold it into four thicknesses, and lay it over the design element (barn, house, or tree) you are hooking with that colour. If the folded fabric generously fits over the area, that is how much wool you need for that element.

How do I set up my frame or hoop?

1. Stretch your backing material over the frame/hoop while tightening the frame to hold the material in place and keep the surface taut, like a drum. This will make it easier to pull the loops through the backing than if the material were loose.

2. Sit comfortably in a chair, resting the hoop or frame in your lap. Be sure to have good lighting and a small table nearby for your wool and supplies.

Where in my picture do I start to hook?

Select a design element (house, barn, animal, or tree) in the centre of your picture. Start with size #5 or #6 cut wool strips. Outline the element first, then fill it in.

(Note: The following instructions are for right-handed people; switch hands if you are left-handed.)

1.   Place one wool strip in your left hand, stretched from between your third finger and thumb to between your first two fingers. Hold left hand under the taut surface of the backing material (see photo).

2.   Hook from the top to the bottom on the outline of your selected element. Hold your hook comfortably in your right hand. Push the hook tip down through the backing material, letting the shaft spread the fibres to enlarge the hole. This will prevent the tip of the hook catching on the square hole, and the wool strip will slide more easily through the hole in the backing.

3. Maneuvre the handle so the tip of the hook, nose up, collects the stretched wool strip from between your fingers, then gently pull the wool up through the hole in the backing to the top.

4. Pull the strip up so one end of it (the tail) is sticking upward. Leave the tail about ½ inch (1 cm) long.

5. As you pull up the wool strip with the hook, continue to hold the strip between your fingers below the backing, allowing the strip to slide through your fingers. This will keep the strip flat and prevent it from twisting, which would create a lump on the back of your work.

6. Following the outline of the element in the pattern, push the hook down through the next square hole in the backing.

7. Again, maneuvre the tip of the hook to collect the wool strip stretched between your thumb and fingers, and pull the loop up through the backing to the top, bringing the loop up to the same height as the width of your wool strip for size #5 or #6 cut wool. This will be ⁵⁄₃₂ or ³⁄₁₆ inches (just less than ½ cm) in height.

8. Repeat. To prevent pulling excessively on or pulling out the previous loop, when you draw up the next loop, roll the hook back onto the previous loop (i.e., pull it a little farther than the previous loop), allowing the strip to slide through the fingers of your left hand. With the hand below the backing, you can adjust the height of your loops by pulling down slightly on the wool strip to match the height of the other loops.

9. Hook three square holes then skip one hole, hook three holes, skip a hole. Or hook two holes, skip a hole, hook two holes, skip a hole, and so on, whichever has the best tension between the loops. Skipping a hole will prevent "packing" (see glossary) and ensure the loops lie flat.

10. Using your chosen pattern (i.e., hook three, skip one, or hook two, skip one), follow the outline of the element in your pattern by continuing to pull the loops up until approximately ½ inch (1 cm) of the wool strip is left.

THE GARRETT BLUENOSE PATTERNS

11. Insert the hook into the next hole, letting the shaft spread the fibres to enlarge the hole, and bring up the tip of your hook with the wool strip on it, pulling the loop up through the backing. Continue to pull it up until the end (the tail) is up.

12. Take a new strip of wool and place it in position in the left hand as before, stretched between your fingers and thumb, holding it under the backing.

13. Push the tip of the hook down through the same square hole that the single tail is in.

14. Maneuvre the handle so the tip of the hook collects the stretched wool strip between your fingers and pull the wool strip up through the backing to the top, continuing to pull until you have a tail ½ inch (1 cm) long in the same square hole with the previous tail.

15. Trim both tails to the same height as the loops.

16. Continue bringing up loops in this fashion until the outline is complete. Now you're ready to fill in the centre of the element.

How do I fill in the side of my house (a square element)?

1. Select one colour of wool strip for this element, and place it in your left hand, stretched between your thumb and fingers, below the backing material.

2. You will be hooking the rows running parallel to the outline. Turn your frame so you are working toward yourself, and place your hook tip at one end of the row of square holes next to your outline, at the very first open hole.

3. Insert the hook tip through backing material, top to bottom, in the very first hole of the first row in your selected element.

4. Following the same hooking instructions as for the outline, follow that straight line of holes (the trench) to complete the row next to the outline.

5. In the last hole of the row, insert the tip of your hook and bring up the single tail.

6.   Trim the tail to the same height as the loops. You have completed one straight row.

7.   Depending on the width of the wool strip, you may need to leave some space so the wool lies flat. If that's the case, hook two rows consecutively, skip a row, then hook the very next row. The wool will push over the previous row so there won't be any backing showing through.

8.   Complete each row (leaving blank rows as needed) until the side of the house is filled in.

You have worked hard! Remember to take a break and stretch out your hand, neck, and shoulders.

How do I hook the corner of a box (two straight sides), like a side of the house meeting the roofline?

1.   Follow the outline of the side, hooking the loops consecutively along the trench of the backing. When you get approximately ¾ inch (2 cm) from the end of the row, stop this wool strip, bringing the tail up through the backing.

2.   Start the new wool strip in the same hole as the previous tail so you have two tails in the same square hole.

3.   Trim the ends of the two tails to match the height of the loops.

4.   Continue to hook the straight line to the corner hole where the two straight lines join.

5.   Pull up the loop in the corner position, then move along, pulling up loops on the new straight line. This gives you a nice clean corner without two tails there.

6.   Continue until the wool strip is done, ending with the single tail coming up to the top.

How do I hook circles (like the sun or a ball)?

1. Start with a wool strip and hook following the outline of the circle element until you reach the square hole where the first tail is.

2. In this hole, insert the tip of your hook and bring up a single tail, in the same hole as the first tail.

3. The outline of the circle is complete, and now you can trim the tails to the same height as the loops.

4. Filling the circle can be done in two ways:

   a) Start at the centre and work toward the outline. At the centre, hook three loops in a tight heart shape. Hook the next circle around the three loops. Stop and trim tails. Continue to hook the next circle, then the next circle, moving outward toward the outline.

   b) Start at the outline and work in toward the centre. Following the outline, hook the next circle inside and next to the outline. Stop and trim tails. Continue the next circle inward, gradually making each row (circle) smaller and smaller until the circle is almost filled in. The last "row" is three loops in the shape of a heart in the centre.

How do I hook on the angles, say for a roof pitch?

Hooking angles can be challenging because you are not following the trenches in the backing material. On the diagonal, hook loops in the holes, following the lines of the pattern as best as you can. The loops will travel in a step-like pattern, and you will miss holes in order to achieve a diagonal line with your wool strip. The line will not appear straight, but when you complete hooking on both sides of this line, it will appear to be straighter. Not having all holes filled in gives the appearance of a straight line on the diagonal.

How do I hook curves, say for an evergreen tree or a cat?

1. Start hooking loops at an end, following the outline of the element.

2. Turn your frame as you work, so you are always working toward yourself.

3. Hook loops in the holes, following the lines of the pattern as best as you can.

4. Follow the contours of the shape to create the curves. Keep in mind the shape you are creating. On an evergreen tree, the boughs are horizontal and curved, so hook your loops to follow those lines. A cat has curves going vertically down its back, so hook your loops creating vertical curves. You will do straight areas moving into curved areas until you have outlined the shape completely.

5. Do not hook loops in every hole.

6. To fill in the shape, start the next row just inside the outline and follow the contours of the outline.

7. Continue to fill in the shape, following the contours.

Have I finished my rug? What is left to do?

1. Sign and date your work, using loops in a contrasting colour. Don't place the letters too close together, as they will be difficult to read. Hook the loops slightly higher than the other loops, so the signature will be clear.

2. The top of your mat should not have any open areas through which you can see the backing. Fill in any open areas.

3. All tails should be trimmed neatly to the same height as the loops.

4. The back of the mat should be just as neat as the front and should be smooth and free of tails, lumps, or crossover strips of wool. For a floor rug, a smooth underside means there won't be any noticeable lumps when walking on it.

5. Trim any loose threads to tidy up the appearance.

6. There are various ways to finish the edge of your beautiful mat. As described elsewhere in this manual, many techniques are available: binding, whipping, or framing, or creating a herringbone edge, a braided or crochet edge, or an "Eaton edge." Choose the finishing method best suited to your mat's use, whether it's a table mat, a floor rug, or a piece to hang on the wall. For example, a floor rug requires a finish that is functional and can withstand wear and tear. For wall hangings, you might want a more decorative edge.

7. Be sure to stitch very close to your hooking, all the way around your project, using the zigzag stitch on your sewing machine. Depending on your finish, the excess backing should be cut off one inch out from the zigzag stitch.

8. Pressing your rug (as described in the next chapter) is a very important step that completes the look of all your hard work.

Basic Techniques and Helpful Hints

- Hook what you love and use the colours you love!

- In planning your picture, decide where the light source (the sun or a lamp) will be, and keep this in mind as you select your colours and hook areas of highlight versus shadows.

- When selecting your wool, lay your backing with the pattern on the floor and place the wool fabric you have selected onto your pattern to see if all the colours work well together. As prominent rug hooking teacher Carol Harvey-Clark used to say, "squint your eyes and look at the wool. The colour that does not fit with the others will stand out, then you can replace it with another colour."

- Choose your background colour first, then contrast and complement the colours for the elements (barn, house, tree) with the background colour.

- Try to place a colour in three places in your picture to allow the viewer's eyes to flow through the scene. This is called the artist's triangle of colour.

- Keep in mind that dark colours recede, and light or bright colours come forward.

- Always hook toward yourself. Turn your frame or hoop as you work to maintain this position.

- If you are right-handed, work left to right so you are inserting the hook through empty backing and not over completed work. If left-handed, work right to left.

- Do not carry a strip over a couple of holes as this will add a lump to the underside, creating an area of wear on the rug and a lump to walk on.

- Remember to push the hook tip through the backing material, letting the shaft spread the fibres to enlarge the hole. This will prevent the tip of the hook from catching on the square hole, and the wool strip will slide through the hole in the backing more easily.

- To prevent pulling excessively on or pulling out the previous wool strip loop, when drawing up the loop, roll the hook back onto the previous loops, allowing the strip to slide through your fingers.

- Don't hook every square hole and every row because your work will be too tight and will want to roll, not stay flat. Instead, hook three square holes then skip one, hook three holes then skip one, or try hooking two holes then skipping one, to see which fits better and is not too tight. Also, hook two rows then skip a row. When you resume hooking on the next row, it will push back over the previous row, and the backing will not be visible.

- As you work, trim tails to the same height as your loops.

- Every twenty minutes or so, take a break and relax your hooking hand, neck, and shoulders. Stretching exercises are helpful to ensure your muscles will not be sore and overworked.

- Just marvel how the various stunning wools are appearing in your project. Plaid doesn't look the same after you hook it. Dip dyes and spot dyes create such beautiful effects!

- Enjoy the process and have fun. You are a rug hooker now!

THE GARRETT BLUENOSE PATTERNS

SOURCES

In addition to the following sources, the author drew inspiration from three rug hooking courses:

"Buildings with Landscapes" taught by Ruth Downing at the Rug Hooking Museum of North America, Hubbards, NS, in 2017; a course with Carol Harvey-Clark at Spruce Top Rug Hooking Studio, Mahone Bay, NS, 2018; and "Learning How to Hook a Rug," a presentation given by Jane Holden in Teacher Training at the Rug Hooking Guild of Nova Scotia Rug School, Halifax, 2019.

Hrkman, Donna. "An Intro to Rug Hooking for Beginners." rughookingmagazine.com/Rug-Hooking-Articles/An-Intro-to-Rug-Hooking-for-Beginners. 2017.

Jewet, Nancy. "Red Bone Doggy." *Rug Hooking Magazine*, Jan.–Feb. 2007, 23–26.

Moshimer, Joan. Basic How to Hook Directions. Handout. Date unknown.

Olsen, Jane. *The Rug Hooker's Bible*. Mechanicsburg, PA: Stackpole Books, 2005.

Pierce, Laura W. "1 Padula, 2 Padula, 3 Padula Fun." *Rug Hooking Magazine*, Sept.–Oct. 2008, 12–16.

A Compilation of Tips and Tricks

Janet Delo

With thanks to contributors Elizabeth Bastin, Celia Charlton, Janet Delo, Ruth Downing, Dwight Gallagher, Mary Grant, Doris Norman, and Anne Lockhart. With information from teachers Anne Boissinet, Germaine James, Cindy MacIntosh, and Muriel Peveril.

Words of Wisdom

- Continue to learn—take a class, learn a new technique, try a different style of hooking, try hooking with a different material. There is always something new to learn.

- Hook and share with fellow hookers—a great way to be inspired or be an inspiration. Have fun!

- There is only one basic tip for rug hooking: do what you love and love what you do. There really are no rules, only suggestions.

- Don't let others choose your colours and textures; hook what YOU like. Remember, it is your mat and you have to like it.

Hooks

- The two purposes of a hook are to spread the threads of the background to handle the width of the wool strip and to guide the loop from the back of the piece to the front.

- Insert the hook fully into the backing and even wiggle it a little to open the hole enough to make pulling the loop easier.

- Use the hook to pull the loop slightly higher than you want, then tug gently on the wool from the back to bring it to the right height.

- The hook must be comfortable in your hand. Try to hold it in the palm of your hand, as it is easier on your wrist.

- Never buy a hook until you have tried it.

- Avoid holding the hook too tightly; this will increase your fatigue.

Frames and Cutters

- When using a frame with gripper strips, once your backing is in place, cover the edges with a terry towel, quilted fabric, or a split paint roller to preserve the integrity of your skin.

- When transporting a frame with gripper strips or carpet-tack strips, use a protective covering so it does not catch on other items you are transporting.

- Always remove your work from the frame when you are finished hooking for the day. This will prevent strain on the backing.

- Gripper strips work best when the backing is not burlap. Use of a split paint roller will protect your arms and also hold the backing firm.

- To extend the life of your cutter, use 100 percent wool; cut other materials by hand.

- Before cutting wool with your cutter, tear it into two- or three-inch strips so that it is easier to hold in place for a more even and straighter cut.

- There are many types of frames on the market; try them out before you buy one. The same rule of thumb applies to cutters. Both of these tools are expensive and are an investment that will serve you for many years.

Backings

- In order to prevent wear on the backing, roll it instead of folding it.

- Many of the backing materials have extra fibres that may come to the front of your work. To remove them, brush the piece gently with a nylon brush, bath mitt, or lint roller.

- Keep backing taut in the frame. This will give you better tension, and your work will show it. When drawing on your backing, always use a marker that is permanent on fabric. Sharpies and Sharpie Rub-a-Dub fabric markers are good for this.

- When drawing a straight line on your fabric, use a pencil to mark "in the ditch" (see glossary). Carpenters' pencils work very well.

Scissors

- Bent-handle (offset) scissors allow the blades to be kept flat against your work and will give a more even cut.

- Always keep your scissors sharp.

- Lee Valley rare earth magnets placed on a gripper strip frame are a convenient place for your scissors.

Wool

- Wool content can be tested in a number of ways. Soaking in bleach will completely dissolve 100 percent wool; if fibres are left behind, the fabric contains synthetic material. If wool is burned, there will be ash residue, and if rubbed on your cheek, wool will feel soft. When torn, it will have a soft sound.

- Store wool in breathable containers, otherwise, it will change colour and deteriorate. Zipper-lock produce bags work well for strips and yarn.

- When purchasing wool, look at the twist in the fibre. If it is tightly twisted, as in worsted cloth, it will not fluff up and will shred when you hook.

- If you are hooking a floor mat, you may want to stick to 100 percent wool and include no embellishments (see glossary).

- Moths do not like sun and suds. Wash all reclaimed wool in hot water and soap. In the spring or summer, unfold your wool and expose it to sun and air.

- Hold wool up to the light to see how open the weave is. If you see a lot of light, the weave is loose and will not hook well in a fine cut. Number 5 cut or higher would be good for open weave, and #4 and lower for a tighter weave.

- Ripping wool weakens the weave, so take care. Make your cut and then gently tear, holding the fabric away from your body in both hands and pulling one hand up along the opposite arm to the shoulder. Tear until close to the end, and then use scissors to snip the last little bit. It is all in the arm action.

Dyeing

- Always start with clean, washed fabric.

- If the material is dark and may run in the wash, soak the fabric in soapy water for 25 minutes. The colour will run. Then add vinegar and simmer for 45 to 60 minutes to fix the colour. Leaving the material without stirring will allow for an uneven absorption, which will be more interesting to hook.

- Over-dyeing small checkered or plaid fabric of any colour with yellow, brown, or green makes for great flower centres.

- When dip-dyeing, sew a basting stitch through the wool to be dyed at ⅓ and ⅔ intervals. This is easier than eyeballing to get the proportions of colour required.

- Baking soda will leach out the colour of fabrics that will run; vinegar will set the dye if you are adding more; and salt will smooth out the colour.

- A wetting agent such as Jet-Dry dishwasher rinse agent will help open the fibres to accept the dye.

- You should not use your everyday cooking utensils for dyeing.

- Bend the shanks of spoons for easier measuring.

- Not all measuring cups and spoons are created equal. Be consistent and use the same implements all the time.

- Clean dye spoons in a glass jar containing coarse salt. Keep three separate jars: reds, blues, and yellows. When the jars become coloured with dye, use them to dye fabric. The mordant will already be in the dye. Sprinkle this on wet fabric for interesting results.

- Never boil wool. When dyeing wool, put it in tepid water and bring it to a boil, then simmer. Boiling will denature the protein in the wool, and your wool strips will break easily. Wool has natural lanolin in it. To allow dye to "take," always pre-soak the wool first in water with several drops of Jet-Dry or another wetting agent for about twelve hours. This will assist the absorption of the dye into the wool.

Loops and Hooking

- Do the stay-stitching on the pattern before you start to hook. If you leave it until you are finished hooking, the piece could be very heavy and awkward to handle with a sewing machine.

- The height of the loop is a personal choice. As a rule of thumb, the height should be the same height as the width of the strip you are using. Hold a strip on edge beside your hooking to check this.

- If you are using various widths of strips, choose one height and stick to it.

- The outer edge of your piece should have slightly lower loop-height than in the rest of your piece. This will make a nice edging.

- To help to keep loops the same height, pull the loop with your hook slightly higher than needed, then pull gently back with your other hand until the loop is the right height.

- To "hide" the tails of your hooking, give them a slight tug when you are clipping them. They will relax and hide back between the loops of your hooking.

- Hold the wool strip under your piece quite close to the back side. This will keep the tension more even.

- Avoid crowding loops, known as "packing." That said, the work should not show blank spaces when taken off the frame and placed on a flat table.

- The amount of wool needed to cover an area will depend on the cut. A three- or four-cut will require about four times the amount of wool; larger cuts will require five or six times the amount. Fold the wool you intend to use in four (or six) and see if it covers the area on which it is to be used.

- When hooking rows side by side, hook so that the barb on the hook is pointing away from the previous row. This way the barb will not get caught in the previous row. (This will not entirely work when doing a fill-in.)

- When you have a contour, hook in the shape of the contour.

- Do not "cross over." If you come up to a loop and want to hook on the other side of it, clip the strip and start on the other side. Crossovers will wear out faster than the other parts of your mat.

- Check the back of your mat periodically and ensure that it is neat. There should be no twists in your strip and no crossovers.

- When you are just about finished, turn your work over and mark "holidays" (bare spots that need to be filled in) with toothpicks. When you turn your work right-side up, you will be able to see what needs to be finished.

- If you come to a difficult spot when filling in, clip the strip and start again, even if you are only doing a tail, a loop or two, and a tail.

- When turning a corner, hook the last three or four holes to the corner with no skips. Turn your hook at a right angle, skip one hole, and then hook three or four with no skips.

- When making a pointed star, find the middle of your strip and use that to hook the point, then hook at right angles on either side of the point.

- Hooking letters and numbers: always hook your letters or numbers first. Often the letters seem to "sink" into the surrounding hooking. Hook the background around them. If the words are unclear or difficult to read, pull them out and rehook. Your holes will be there to hook into, and you will automatically pull them up higher. Always have someone who does not know what you have written read it. If another person struggles to read it, you need to rehook all or some of the lettering.

- If you are able to hook a tail, a loop, and a tail out of that piece of wool strip, hook it in the mat—don't throw it away!

Fine Shading

- Pick swatches with good gradation—no big jumps between values.

- Middle values tend to be used more quickly in hooking flowers. Don't waste! Purchase two swatches for larger flowers to be on the safe side.

- When cutting your swatches, keep them contained and separated with a cardboard or plastic divider and elastic. Some values are so close in colour that it is sometimes hard to differentiate without the dividers.

- Hook inside the line of your flowers as they can bulge and expand quickly.

- There are no straight lines in Mother Nature! Always hook with a curve or a bend in your flowers or leaves. If you do have a straight line, squeeze an end-loop-end (also referred to as tail-loop-tail) against the line, and it will create a wave.

- Always stagger your tails in fine shading. It will produce a smoother transition between values and a more pleasing appearance.

- In nature, there is imperfection. No two leaves or petals are exactly the same. Vary your shapes and colours to add diversity and interest in your rug.

- If your swatch is light-coloured and you don't have enough separation between petals, hook a fine line with embroidery floss or a #2 cut in an appropriate darker shade to help create that definition.

- Hook what is on top first, in lighter values, whether leaves or petals. For the motif underneath, create depth and contrast with shadows in the darkest values.

- Follow the contours of your flowers and leaves from the base out toward the tip.

- If you need a fleck of colour in a hooked flower, use your hook and thumbnail to work the loops into your hooking.

Design and Colour Planning

- When a design or drawing is done on a square or rectangular linen or burlap backing, it is important that the backing be properly squared off. This will ensure that the corners of your mat are square and that each side is exactly the same as the opposite side and the pattern is straight on the grain. Before drawing in the ditch, pull out one single thread on each side of the backing and then draw the outline in each of the ditches you have created.

- When you are hooking a design, hook on the inside of the marking on your backing. If you hook on the line or outside it, the design will be larger than you expect.

- It is usually helpful to hook one line of background around your design as you are doing it. This will keep your design in good shape.

- Usually, you hook what is "in front" first and work your way to the background.

- There are a number of ways to place your design/pattern on the backing. You may transfer the pattern "with designer's permission," using either red dot (see glossary), see-through materials such as tulle, fine grey screening, or a transparency and overhead.

- Use the triangle of colour when doing a pictorial. Your scene will look balanced. When hooking a colour, make sure it appears in three corners, either as the same colour, more muted, or bolder.

- Stand back and study your piece quite often for proper perspective and to coordinate colours. Using a door peeper (see glossary) is also good for studying detail. If something is out of place, either in your hooking or in a colour you have chosen, it will show up. Holding your piece in front of a mirror will also reflect details or colours out of place.

- Following a fundamental technique in drawing and painting of a pictorial scene, hook objects or elements in groups of threes and fives instead of even numbers.

Whipping, Finishing, and Storing

- Keep a photographic record of completed mats with an accompanying record of all pertinent information that you might want for future reference.

- Store wool following the colour wheel, and use ventilated clear containers, storage bins, or shelving that allow you to see what you actually have. Ventilation holes can be easily drilled in most plastic containers.

- To determine the amount of yarn needed to whip your mat, estimate ten feet of washed and shrunk yarn for every inch of the circumference of your mat.

- To ensure that your whipping will be even, whip about one inch of the mat, then take that out and determine the width of the background needed for the whipping. Mark your mat at this distance. If the mat is a rectangle, you can count the numbers of holes between the hooked part and the whipping line. On curves, it is easiest to mark with a dressmaking ruler that has a slide to keep the measurement equal.

- When you are finished your work, it is a good idea to press it using a steam iron and a wet towel. Do not slide the iron but press it on the rug until it no longer makes a sound.

- There are a number of ways to finish a rug. Some people just turn the backing over, some use cording and whip-stitch with yarn; some cut and roll the backing forward and whip stitch, some crochet the binding.

- If your mat is going to be on the floor, the edges should be whipped for longer wear.

- Mats that are being stored should be rolled with the loops on the outside. Never fold your mat, as it can break the backing over time.

- Stored mats should not be wrapped in plastic; they need to breathe. Old pillowcases are ideal for storage purposes.

- Clover Wonder Clips, commonly used by quilters, are a great help in holding your cording while doing your whipping. They are wonderful on corners and are a real time-saver.

- Finished mats can go in the dryer on "air" for twenty minutes, and you won't believe the amount of lint, pet hair, etc. that comes out of them. The same can be said for strips placed in a lingerie bag; a lot of excess lint comes out before you start to hook. Don't forget to clean your dryer lint trap.

Landscapes and Pictorials

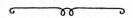

Dwight Gallagher

Most Bluenose or Garrett patterns were hooked in the primitive style of rug hooking, using the materials that were at hand and the colours that were available. The following is a brief outline describing how to hook a landscape mat to give it a three-dimensional effect. Elements within the mat are hooked with three values—light, medium, and dark. The medium value is used for the main colour, the light for the highlight, and the dark for the shade value, giving the finished mat a more interesting effect. Solid-coloured, abrashed-coloured, spot-dyed, and textured material can all be used as long as they are divided into the three values.

Here are three things you should consider first when hooking a landscape pattern:

1. Which season do you want to depict? The colours of the grass and trees in the spring are different from those in the summer and autumn.
2. What type and time of day do you wish to depict? The colour of the sky suggests the time (morning, midday, sunset, night) or type of day (overcast, sunny, rainy).
3. What direction is the light source coming from in your design? This will help you with value placement in deciding shadows and highlights.

Buildings

If your design has a building, it should be hooked first. Begin with the roof and hook it using directional hooking, the way the shingles, tiles, etc. would normally lie. The colour of the roof should be darker than the building colour itself, or vice versa. A darker value of the colour used in the roof can be used on the edge of the roof and under the eaves to give a contrast.

We usually only see two sides of a chimney, and one side should be hooked with a darker-coloured value, depending on the direction of the light source. Bricks are hooked in a horizontal direction, but a cement chimney is hooked vertically. Hook a shadow line where the roof and chimney meet to "ground" the chimney on the roof. Should there be smoke coming from the chimney? You decide!

Outline the door- and window frames with a contrasting colour to that used for the main building. Hook an L-shaped shadow line inside the door- and window casing, giving dimension to the features. Hook the door in a vertical direction, choosing the design of the door: is it plain or decorative? Does it have a window or a wreath hanging on it? Don't forget the doorknob! When you hook the windows, decide if there is a light source coming from the inside of the building, or if there is a reflection of the sky on the windowpanes. Reverse hooking works great for windows!

The sides of the building itself are usually hooked in a horizontal direction, with one side of the building being a darker-coloured value, depending on the direction of the light source. Remember to coordinate the dark side of the building with the dark side of the chimney. Are there shrubs, small bushes, or flowers around the building? If not, consider placing a shadow line around the base of the building, anchoring the building to the foreground (see diagram #1).

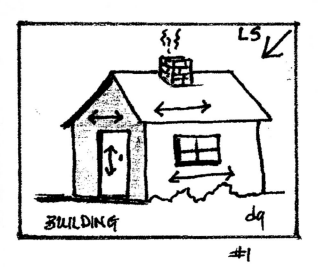

Foreground

If there is a definite horizon line in your design, hook it first. If it's where water meets the sky, place a straight line of hooking to set the horizon.

Consider dividing the foreground into three sections, using a different value of the colour in each section. Your brightest/darkest colour should be in the front of the landscape, with the lightest value toward the back or closest to the horizon, leaving the medium value for the middle section. The colours of the foreground get lighter as they get closer to the horizon line, which gives perspective to the landscape. Do not hook everything in straight horizontal lines— use directional hooking to form hills, clumps of grass, etc., giving interest and movement to the

foreground. Where the sections of the foreground meet, "finger in" (see "fingering" in the glossary) some of the colour from the next section to soften the transition. Don't forget to add shadows under trees and shrubs and other elements in the design, depending on the direction of the light source (see diagram #2).

Trees

When you have trees in your design, you should hook the trunk of the tree first and in a vertical direction. Hook one edge with a darker value giving a shade effect; the light value should be hooked on the opposite side; medium values hooked in the middle. Finger in the values, stagger your tails, and mix different shades of the colour, all adding interest to the tree trunk. Tree trunks decrease in size as they ascend, and remember to carry the three-value hooking technique into the tree limbs.

If the trees in your landscape have leaves, determine the season, and hook with colour values in relationship to the season. Consider hooking the leaves in irregular-shaped clusters, not as individual leaves. Use lighter values at the higher and outer tips of the cluster, darker values at the bottom and closer to the trunk of the cluster, and fill in with the medium values. To give a realistic effect, add "sky holes" where the sky is peeking through several areas of the leaf cluster.

Evergreen trees keep their colour all year long and do not announce the season unless there is snow on their branches. Starting at the top of the tree and hooking down the trunk, hook the evergreen branch with curved lines following the direction of the needle growth. Use three values of the colour: light for highlights on the branch tips, a darker value for underneath the branch and closer to the trunk, and medium for the main part of the branch. The side of the tree opposite to the light source will have fewer highlights. Hook small sections of the visible tree trunk as you descend, and add small sections of the sky colour between the branches—but do not overdo either of the two.

If hooking a group of evergreen trees, the trees closer to the horizon are of a lighter colour value. The treetops in the group of evergreens should never be at the same height. Trees in the distance should be shorter and lighter in colour (see diagrams #3, #4, #5, and #8).

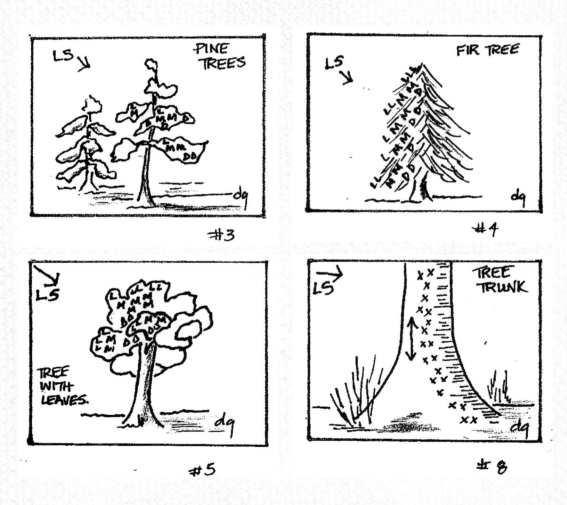

Skies

The mood of your landscape, the time of day, and the season are all reflected in the sky. Summer skies tend to be bright in colour, whereas autumn skies are a bit more muted, and winter skies tend to be a shade of grey. Skies at sunrise are often a pastel colour near the horizon (pink, light blue, peach) compared with the brilliant colours (reds, oranges, purples) of the sunset. A quiet, simple sky works well with a busy picture, but a more reserved scene can benefit from an exciting sky.

#6

The sky closer to the horizon is lighter in colour and gets more vibrant moving upward. Consider dividing the sky area into three sections and hooking each section with a different value of the same colour. Use the fingering technique of hooking where the sections meet (see Mary Grant's chapter for an explanation of fingering technique); combining the colours avoids a definite straight line of division.

Skies are usually hooked horizontally; you can create movement in the sky by hooking in slightly curved lines. Hook your sky vertically if you are using a painted piece of fabric.

Cumulus clouds are the most common cloud formation we see hooked in skies. They are larger and puffier the closer they are to us, and smaller and flatter the farther away they are. Cumulus clouds are composed of sections that appear piled on each other and are hooked with curved lines. Create shadows and highlights within the cloud formation and at the base of the cloud with a grey or a purple. Clouds look best hooked with small tails that extend into the sky around them.

If you are hooking or adding flying birds to the design, remember that the birds flying closer to you are larger than the ones in the distance. Clouds and birds should appear in odd numbers, which is artistically pleasing to the eye (see diagram #6).

Rocks

Rocks are rarely the focal point of a design and are usually hooked in a subdued colour palette of browns and greys, but greens and blues add interest to the finished element. Solid, spot-dyed, and tweed materials work great for hooking rocks. Cracks and crevices should be hooked in darker colours—but not black.

Whether the rock is smooth or rough with sharp edges, its surface can be divided into sections or faces, and each is hooked individually. Alter the direction in which you hook each section. Determine the direction of your light source and select the colour value for each

#7

section accordingly—lighter colours where it hits the section directly, darker colours for sections used for shading the rock and near the base.

Hook sprigs of grass, smaller rocks, or shadow lines at the base of the rock to "ground" it on the surface (see diagram #7).

Water

When hooking water in your design, consider these things:

1. Water reflects its surroundings (sky, trees, depth) and takes on colour from them.

2. Water is moving; do not hook in perfectly straight lines—give it movement.

3. Water does not always have to be blue.

The colour of the water should be darker than what you use for the sky. The water colour should be brighter closest to you and lighter as it recedes toward the horizon. Where the water is the deepest (e.g., the middle of a lake), hook a few darker strips to denote depth. If there are whitecaps on the water, they get narrower in size and shorter in length as they recede toward the horizon. Bring some sky colour into the water, especially when hooking sunsets and sunrises.

A river or stream narrows and usually bends as it recedes toward the horizon. Anchor the sides of your river or stream to the land by hooking with a darker colour value.

The best advice is to look at the elements in nature more closely. Consider the direction of the light source and study the colours, shadows, and highlights. Take a mental picture of what you want to hook, and hook away.

Most importantly, have fun!

SOURCES

Green, Jane Halliwell. *Pictorial Hooked Rugs*. Stackpole Magazines, 2009.

Garrett's Seascapes

Anne Lockhart

What would the famous Bluenose Patterns be without pictures of that famous ship and the seascape around it? The patterns are iconic. How do we, as rug hookers, make them our own while acknowledging the past? As I write this, I am thinking of the many students who took the class at the 2019 AGM. The chair pads were amazing and all so very different. Many were hooked realistically, but in others, it was a case of "anything goes."

If the ship is the focal point of your rug, do it first. For the mat shown below, I started with the rigging. I often use variegated yarn or a spot dye. You probably would not want it a solid line. In many of the Garrett patterns, the ship is sitting on the water. I was using a dip dye for the sky and didn't have enough of it, so I raised the waterline to make a distant horizon. The horizon of water is always straight. I added some colour for the tops of the waves in the foreground. Notice the flag is going the wrong way. I was too busy worrying about the sails!

If you are looking for realism, you have to decide which direction the wind is blowing and where the sun is shining. Pictures of sailing ships can help. Usually where the sails billow, they are lighter because they are not in the shade. A sail behind another sail would be darker where it is shaded.

Images courtesy of Paul Downing.

I used a dip dye for the sails, but you can create the same effect with swatches. Have fun with the sails. Try using different wools for different effects.

The ocean changes the farther away it is in the picture, with rougher water in the foreground and a straight line at the horizon. If you are hooking a sunset, put some of the colour in the water. If there is a moon, show some refection. The sky is reflected in the water. You will not see turquoise water on a stormy day.

If there is a lighthouse in the picture, you might want to make it realistic. Use a darker shade for the sides and make one side thicker than the other. Make sure the building is grounded with bushes or a bit of dirt so the base of the building is not flat.

Many of the Garrett patterns do not have a lot of detail and were hooked in yarn with a limited amount of colour. We are lucky to have so many colours and fabrics at our fingertips. We can go wild with velvet water, silk skies or sails, roving clouds, and foamy tips of waves, and use many other fabrics and ideas.

Enjoy.

THE GARRETT BLUENOSE PATTERNS

Geometrics

Celia Charlton

Geometric rugs are fun to hook, but it's important that you design, apply your pattern to your backing, and colour-plan before you pick up your hook. All the work goes into the preparation, and if you do it with careful thought and consideration, you'll have a geometric rug that will be dazzling. We are often anxious to get straight to the hooking part, but patience and common sense will ensure that you avoid pitfalls and will make the hooking part fun and rewarding. Once you do the preliminary work, you are left with the fun part.

Choose colours you love. Twenty people can hook the same geometric pattern and produce twenty very different rugs. With geometrics, it's all about colour. Let your geometric rug reflect your personality. Use colours that excite you, and don't be afraid to toss in colours you haven't used before. Push yourself a little and dare to try something different. A geometric rug does not have to have a complicated pattern to be beautiful. The use of colour and values can make simple squares stunning.

Tips for Geometric Application

- Your choice of backing is important. You need an even weave. Some backings have thick and thin threads. You need a backing with uniformity. Choose carefully. I prefer linen. Rug warp is also a good choice.

Threads are not uniform.

Threads are more uniform.

- Check your ruler. Some begin measurement at the end of the ruler. Others begin slightly inside the end. Whichever you choose, be consistent. It's a small space, but can make a big difference if all your measurements are slightly off.

The ruler above shows that the first inch begins about ¼ inch from the left end.

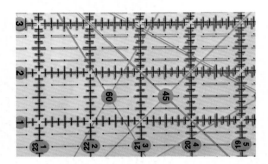

The yellow ruler above begins measurement on the left,
at the very end of the ruler.

- Apply all your markings first with a pencil. A 2HB is best. If your pencil is too hard, you won't see the mark. Run the pencil along the weave of your backing with a slow and steady hand. Go over it again to make sure you've stayed in the groove. Falling even one thread outside the line can make a difference in a geometric, so be precise.

- Does your pattern have a lot of diagonal lines? Take a careful look at your pattern and apply it to the backing so that most of your lines are along the straight weave. It's easier to hook along straight lines, and it reduces the possibility of raised spots in your finished rug that refuse to steam out. A lot of hooking along the uneven grain pushes the threads into an unnatural shape and causes that "wonky" look. This is especially important for those who tend to pack (see definition of "packing" in the glossary).

- Apply your pattern, beginning at the centre of your backing, and work outward, measuring carefully as you go. To find the centre, fold your backing in half, then in quarters, and mark the centre spot. Draw lines straight through the centre in north, south, east, and west directions. This establishes your median point and divides your pattern into quarters. As you apply the pattern, the threads will move ever so slightly, making it important to begin in the centre and have these threads move outward. Beginning on the outside and working toward the centre can push the threads of your backing too close together in the middle. In some patterns (e.g., inch mats), it's best to actually count your backing threads and then mark.

THE GARRETT BLUENOSE PATTERNS

- Make sure you are totally satisfied with your pencil markings before you go over them with a permanent marker. Taking particular care at this stage could save you a lot of frustration later.

- Grid or no grid? Depending on your pattern, you might want to hook a grid line, leave it out entirely, or hook some grid lines and leave out others. Either way, draw the grid lines on the backing. You will need these lines whether you intend to hook on them or beside them. Use different coloured permanent markers: one for grid lines to be hooked, and another for those to be left as a guide only. If you do not want the grid line to show, you must hook INSIDE it. If you want your grid line to show, hook right on the line.

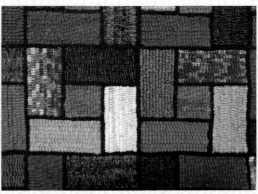

Example of a rug with the grid hooked on the line.
The dark value of the grid line provides contrast, so colour is enhanced.

This rug has been hooked with no grid line to outline the squares.

- Choose your grid line wool colour carefully. Very light and very dark usually make the best grid lines. You can run into problems if you do not have enough contrast when you use medium values; however, if you choose colours carefully, medium grid lines can work.

Take your time, have patience, and plan. It'll be worth it!

Primitive Flowers and Leaves

Doris Norman

The origin of rug hooking is unknown; there is documented evidence that shows fabrics were hooked as far back as the fifth century in Egypt. The Oslo Museum in Norway has examples of hooking made by the Vikings. We know that our great-grandmothers hooked rugs to cover cold floors and to beautify their homes.

There are many beautiful flowers found in the Garrett designs—tubular flowers, flat-petalled flowers, and roses—that lend themselves to being hooked in the shaded and/or the primitive rug hooking style. As well, there are a few "padulas" or imaginary flowers.

"Primitive hooking," also called "hook and fill," refers to the manner in which a mat is hooked. Shapes are outlined with a different fabric or colour from the main (fill) colour; following the contour of the flower/leaf will give it shape. The "fill" may be any fabric or yarn of your chosen colour.

Texture adds dimension and depth to primitive hooked mats. It lifts the mat from a hooked surface to an interesting work of art and encourages the viewer to reach out and touch the surface. Woven tweeds, checks, herringbone, and a variety of cut strip-widths add texture. They may be all muddled together in one dye pot to blend colours, creating an aged, unified appearance.

Primitive chair seat, black and white.

Primitive chair seat, colour.

The hooking of primitive flowers and leaves is quite easy. Following the suggested guidelines in this article will help you get started—then hook, punch, or prod your own style.

Method

The centres of all the flowers are hooked first, using a colour from another part of the design, or the usual yellow or gold.

Flat-petalled Flowers

Flat-petalled flowers (see diagram), such as daisies, pansies, or wild roses, are lettered indicating the easiest hooking order. Petal A is hooked first, as it is fully exposed; B has one side covered by another petal; C has both sides covered by upper petals. Using a dark, duller fabric helps define the overlapped petal.

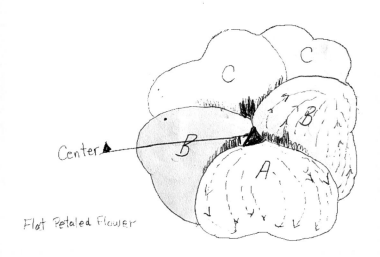

THE GARRETT BLUENOSE PATTERNS

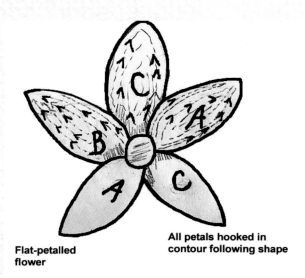

Flat-petalled flower

All petals hooked in contour following shape

These flat-petalled flowers may also be hooked with every other petal using the same outline and fill fabrics in lighter values. The petals under the top petals, where the petals overlap, are hooked in a darker outline and fill fabrics of the same colour family.

Tubular-shaped Flowers

Tubular-shaped flowers (daffodils, lilies, petunias, morning glories, etc.) are hooked somewhat differently.

Hook the centre in a dark value. Outline petals all the way around, and also the throat, in the darkest value of the flower colour. Hook the main colour from centre out to edge; fan out the strips as suggested by arrows. To achieve the tubular appearance, the throat is outlined and filled with the same fabric and colour.

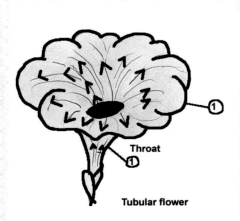

Throat

Tubular flower

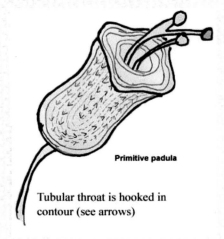

Primitive padula

Tubular throat is hooked in contour (see arrows)

Roses

Roses are found in many of the Garrett designs. They may be hooked in a shaded manner or in a primitive manner. These roses generally have more features than other primitive flowers. They do not have to be all red but may be varieties of gold, ivory, mauve, blue, etc. (See Garrett designs with roses: 2039, 840, 828, and 2123.)

Following the letters, hook one petal at a time. Start with A, which is a dark value, then B, C, D, etc. The numbers indicate where six different fabrics may be placed.

1. Establish the outline of each petal using a different colour or texture than the main flower colour.

2. Hook one row of the main colour after the outline and fill in the petal, following the contour.

3. For the areas marked "xxx," where one petal falls over another, use a darker colour.

4. Continue to fill the petals with texture and colours relating to the fill colour, following the contour of each petal.

5. Choose another fabric to complement the main colour.

6. The centre is either the darkest value of the fill or a dark from another part of the design.

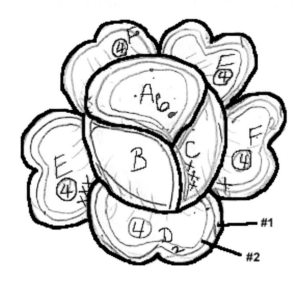

Primitive rose

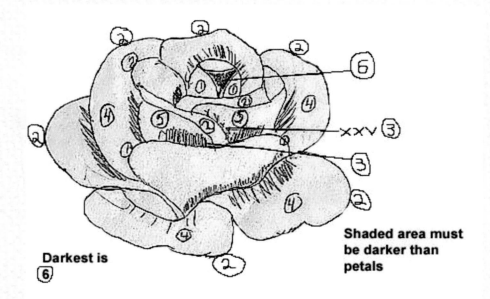

Darkest is
⑥

**Shaded area must
be darker than
petals**

Leaves, Veins, and Stems

Colours found in nature (e.g., red, gold, brown, grey, green) may be used for the leaves. Choose a colour you like that suits the flower, even if it is not in nature. When a large, curved leaf is divided by a vein, it may be hooked in two different values of one colour, with the lighter values on the longer side of the curve. One, two, or three outlines may be used if the leaf is large enough. The last outline should be the fill colour.

When a leaf is partially hidden by another leaf or flower, the leaf underneath should be darker. Very small leaves do not need to be outlined.

Any fabric is suitable for the vein, especially if it is a texture and contrasts with the fill.

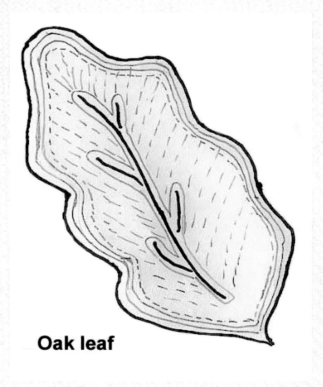

Oak leaf

Illustration of hooking leaf and vein.

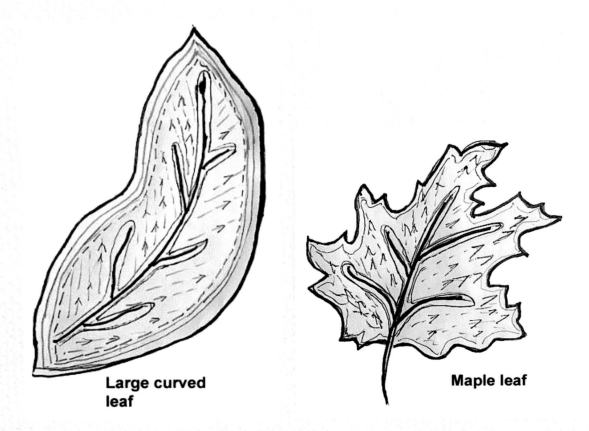

Large curved leaf

Maple leaf

Illustrations of curved leaf and maple leaf (3333). See maple leaf in Garrett design numbers 213, 977, and 2102.

The stem should differ from the vein and should look strong enough to support the leaf or flower.

To hook a leaf:

1. Hook the vein.
2. Hook an outline of the fill all around it.
3. Hook the rest of the leaf with fill from the vein out to meet the fill outline of the leaf.

REFERENCES

Beatty, Alice and Mary Sargent. *Basic Rug Hooking*. Harrisburg, PA: Stackpole Books, 1977.

Moshimer, Joan. *Complete Rug Hooker: A Guide to the Craft*. New York City: Little Brown and Company, 1975.

Three-Colour Shading

Elizabeth Bastin

The purpose of any shading—that is, the blending of different values of a hue or colour—is to create the illusion of dimension, which adds interest to your work. This is true no matter the medium; in this case, we are speaking of rug hooking. Three-value shading is a simple and versatile way to achieve this. The material you use can be specially dyed, or you may be fortunate to have a plaid that will give you these values. Plaids and textured fabrics can create interest and can also be dyed to give the desired effect. Whatever colour you use should complement what is in the rest of the mat.

Let us consider three-value shading for flowers and leaves. Flowers can be broadly categorized into three different shapes: open or flat-petalled (daisy, pansy, wild rose); funnel- or tube-shaped (morning glory, lily); and wraparound (calla lily, multi-petalled rose). The following approach is a suggestion for how to hook these shapes. There are others you can try as well to see how they work for you.

Open-petalled flower

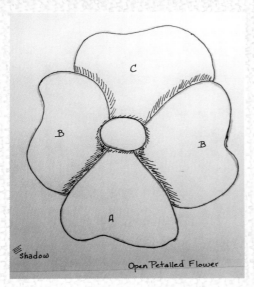
Open Petalled Flower

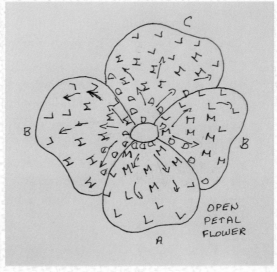
OPEN PETAL FLOWER

Each petal is assigned a letter—A, B, C—that depicts the position of the petal in relation to the others in the shape. Petal A has no other petal on top of it; petal B has one side shadowed by another petal; and petal C has two sides shaded by the adjacent petals. Within each petal, different values can be used to achieve the shadowed effect. It is important to ensure that there is enough contrast between the values along the edge of the flower and the shadowed part of the adjacent petal. Also, hook following the contour of the shape to enhance what the eye sees. Avoid straight-line hooking in a rounded shape. It may be helpful to look at a flower illustration and observe the shading. This applies to all shapes of flowers and leaves.

1. Start with the centre of the flower. Depending on the type of flower, this may be only an end-loop-end, using a contrasting colour. This preserves the shape of the centre.

2. Hook the petal that appears to be on top, i.e., the A petal. Use the darkest value first to hook the area closest to the centre. Stagger the loops to avoid a hard edge when switching values. Switch to the medium value as you hook up the centre of the flower, gradually fanning out toward the edge, but stop short of the edge. Finally, hook with your lightest value to fill in the rest of the petal.

3. When hooking the B petals, the area shadowed by the adjacent petals should be a value darker than the edge of the petal next to it—once again, contrast. The dark value can again be used in the centre of the flower. Using the same principle as with the A petal, work your way up the petal using medium and light values.

4. The same is true for C petals, but you have two shaded sides to consider, all the while staggering the values to give a blended effect. Some petals may have more of one value than the next petal. Think of the effect you wish to achieve. Sometimes it is helpful to draw the flower on paper and shade with a pencil to determine where the light and dark values should be placed.

Tubular flower

1. Start with the centre to maintain the shape.

2. Generally, the throat or inside of the flower is more shaded. It is important to think of how the light hits the flower. One side of the throat may be more shadowed than the rest. Use a dark value to hook around the centre; then, still using the dark value, hook up the side of the tube a short distance, staggering the loops. Once again, switch to your medium and light values to create the illusion of dimension.

3. The area under the top of the flower will be slightly shaded. Also, to create the feeling of a rounded shape, the edges of this part of the flower should be darker, gradually getting lighter toward the middle. Sometimes it is easier to hook this area vertically.

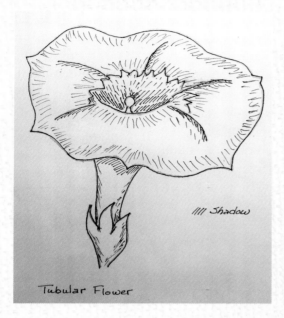

Tubular Flower

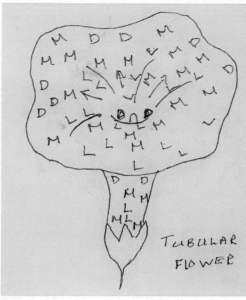

TUBULAR FLOWER

Wraparound flower

1. Start with the centre.

2. As with the tubular flower, hook the area around the centre with the dark value. Gradually switch to medium and light values as you get to the edge of the flower. It is particularly helpful to practice your shading of this shape with a pencil and paper.

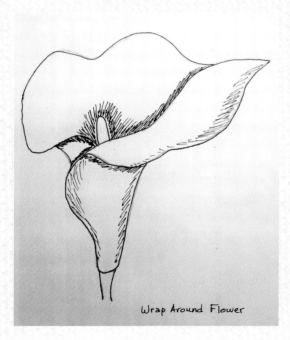

Wrap Around Flower

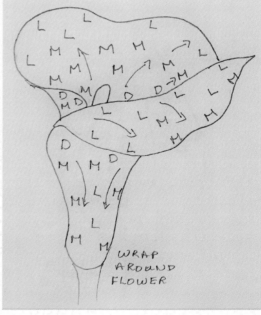

WRAP AROUND FLOWER

Leaves

Leaves can be sorted into three categories: simple oval, multi-lobed, and strap leaves. Once again, it is useful to practice shading leaf shapes to see how these will look when hooked.

Simple oval

1. Hook the vein first, using the same or contrasting colour.

2. On one side of vein, hook the dark value partway along the vein. Switch to the medium value and continue hooking along the side of the vein, keeping to its shape. End before you get to the tip. You may need several rows or partial rows of this value. Fill in the rest of this side with the light value.

3. On the unhooked side of the leaf, hook this space opposite to the way the first side was hooked, i.e., hook the light values along the vein, switch to the medium value, and then to the darkest value.

4. There may be times when you wish to have the dark value on both sides of the vein, working out to light on the edge. This is when practicing on paper may help.

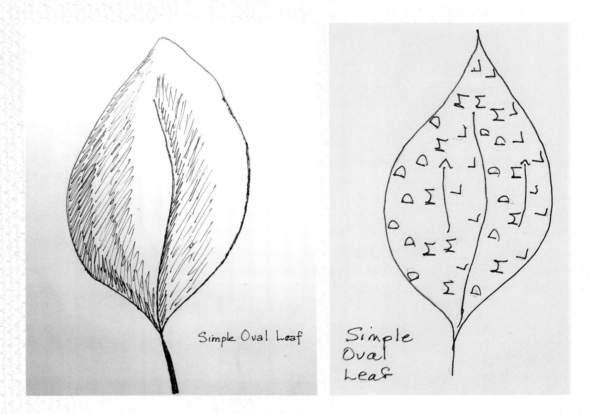

Simple Oval Leaf

Simple Oval Leaf

Multi-lobed leaf

1.   Hook the veins.

2.   Hook the dark value around veins, maybe stopping partway up the leaf. Hook the medium value around the veins the rest of the way. Next, hook the medium value adjacent to the dark value, and then finish with the light value. If you switched to the medium value partway up the leaf, hook the light value next to the medium value.

Multilobed Leaf

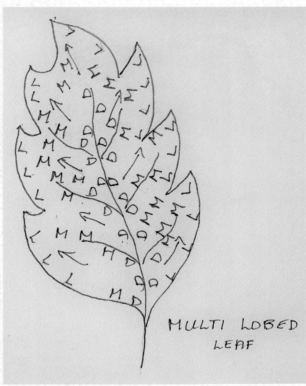

MULTI LOBED LEAF

Strap leaf

1. Hook the vein.

2. As with the oval leaf, hook one side of the leaf from dark to light and the other side from light to dark. With this shape of leaf, the values need to be staggered along the vein, and you will find it necessary to hook more loops of one value before changing to the next value as you near the tip. Once again, it is important to hook following the shape of the leaf.

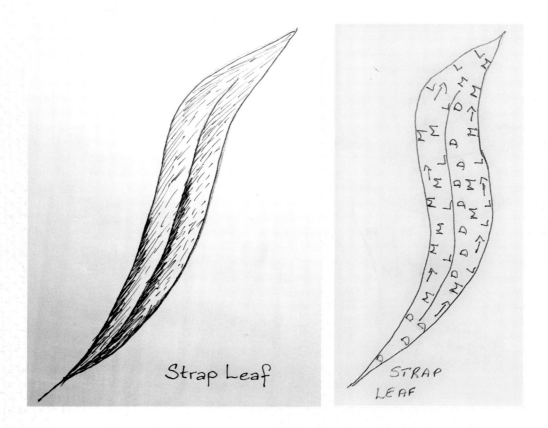

Six-Value Shading of Flowers and Leaves

Mary Grant

The basic principles of shading as applied to three-value and six-value shading are alike; however, their importance merits repetition. The use of different values of a particular hue gives an illusion of three dimensions. In flowers, it adds a sense of depth and height in each individual petal and provides a sense of layering of petals over or under one another. Darker values tend to withdraw or add depth, whereas lighter values will provide the highlight of a slight bulge in a flower or leaf. Whether one petal overlaps another, or a petal or leaf produces a turnover on itself, a shadow is cast. Dark values provide that shadow. In order to distinguish one petal from another, or the edge of a turnover, there should be at least two values between.

It is important to fan out your six-value swatch to ensure that there is a smooth transition from one value to the next with no "jump" between values. If you have a jump, check your stash; you might have something that will fit. There should also be a marked distinction between your darkest and lightest values. When hooking flowers and leaves, it is important to follow the contours of each petal or leaf. I use a number system to distinguish between the six values in a swatch. The numbering convention that I use has #1 as the lightest and #6 as the darkest value. I place these values between two pieces of cardboard, with elastics between each value to separate them, and then I number them.

Flowers

Flowers can be broken down into three main types—open-petalled, funnel- or trumpet-shaped, and wraparound.

Open-petalled: Wild Rose

Start with the flower centre in a contrasting colour or a texture. Centres can vary in size. You can use an end-loop-end (ELE) in a triangular fashion for a small centre. Even with a larger circle, starting with the triangular ELE sets it up to be a rounded shape. Even the centre, especially if it is a button-type centre, will cast a shadow on the petals.

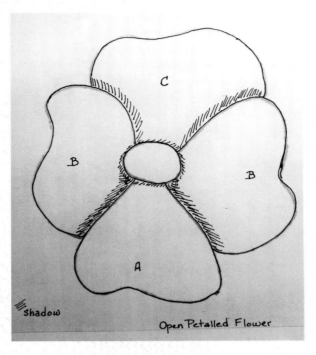

Illustration of lettering petals A, B, C.

There is a common convention of labelling petals to correspond to the amount of shadow on them:

- Petal A is on top of all other petals. This petal casts shadows, but is not in the shadow of any other petal.

- Petal B has one side in the shadow of petal A, but the other side casts a shadow on petals B or C.

- Petal C has both sides in the shadow of the other petals.

Petals are hooked in alphabetical order.

Shading the Petals

- Petal A: Start at the base closest to the flower centre and work out toward the edges. You are aiming for a smooth transition of progressively lighter values. The part closest to the flower centre will be hooked with a #3 value; #2 value will be in the middle area, and #1 toward the edges.

To avoid creating a distinct line between the values, the three values need to be blended. One way to do this is called fingering. Put your hands fingertip to fingertip and open your fingers wide, then slide the fingers on one hand between the fingers on the other hand. This is the basic way in which fingering works. Some values are blended in between the other values.

Starting with value #3, hook curved lines starting at the petal base and curving out along the contour of the petal. The lines will be close together at the base of the petal and widen out as they follow the contour. Depending on the size of the petal, these lines may only be an ELE or an ELLE. Make the lines of different lengths.

With value #2, hook up the sides of the value #3 lines and extend an end or a LE beyond the darker line. Do not be afraid to clip the wool at this point and start a fresh strip on the other side of the darker line. This will keep you from rounding at the ends of the dark lines. If there is a very wide area between the value #2 rows, you can add a line in the middle. Again, be sure to vary the lengths of the lines.

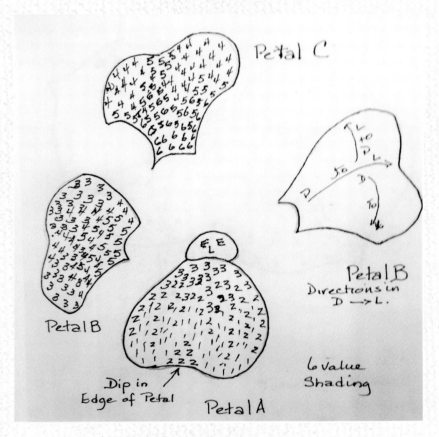

Petal fingering, dip, and direction of shading.

Now take value #1 and hook it up the sides of the value #2 lines, filling in the spaces. If you have kept the contour, you will find the lightest values will start to curl along the edge. Be careful of the side of the petal where it casts a shadow on Petal B. You may wish to bring value #2 deeper into the base of the petal along this side so that the contrast with Petal B where A overlaps it will be easier to achieve.

Note that if there is a "dip" in the edge of a petal, you may choose to emphasize it by hooking a few short lines of the next darker value into the downward curve.

- Petal B follows the same technique, using values #5, #4, and #3 and ensuring that there is a two-value difference where Petal A shadows Petal B, or where one Petal B shades another B. Decisions must be made, as a value #4 next to a value #3 will not distinguish the two petals. It is better to put value #6 or #5 in the shadow and gradually move to value #4 for the darker lines and then a #3 along the far side, which shadows the next B or C petal. The direction of shading from dark to light goes both vertically and horizontally in this case.

- Petal C is shaded on both sides. Value #6 is used at the base and up further on the sides than in the other petals. Values #5 and #4 are added to blend.

Using a sketchpad and coloured pencils is a useful aid to indicate where you need to use each value.

Just a word about highlights. If the petal curves up from the base and then down to the edge, there is an opportunity to show this by adding a highlight in the middle section. Even an ELE or ELLE of the lightest value in the petal where you might otherwise use the middle value will bring a highlight to this spot. Be careful to avoid hooking this in a straight line, though. Try a triangle, much as in the centre of the flower.

Tubular: Morning Glory

This type of flower has a deep throat that tends to disappear down into the centre of the flower. The outer side of the tube is carried on beyond the flatter petal parts.

To create depth, hook the funnel very dark. If there is an opportunity to see more of the interior of the tube, you might want to use value #6 for most of the tube but blend to a value #5 where the light might hit the inside. As you move up from the throat of the flower, you will get lighter and lighter. If it curves under a bit near the outer edge, you may wish to go from medium to the lightest value not quite on the edge, and return to a bit darker on the edge. As with the open-petalled flower, watch where you might want to add an ELE for a highlight, and blend in around it.

The exterior part of the tube is shaded either lighter or darker than the flatter part of the flower, and fingering is used to blend the values. Remember that the contour is greater across the tube than along the length of the tube in order to achieve a rounded effect.

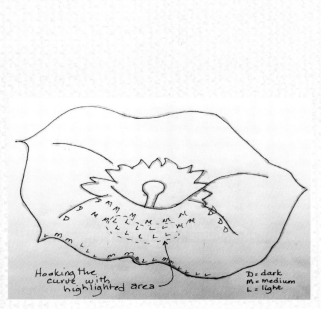

Tubular shading.

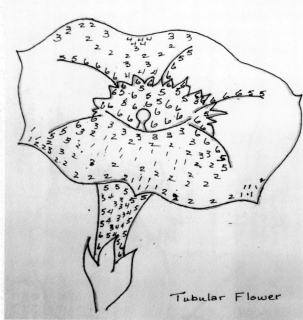

Hooking the curve with highlighted area.

Wraparound: Rose

These flowers tend to have rollovers or turnovers (areas in which the petal turns back on itself). Start with the centre, which is usually done in a darker value. Assess the other petals to see what covers what and therefore where the shadows occur. Use the same fingering technique to ensure that the shadows and the highlights are clear. The rollover tends to be lighter than the rest of the petal and may, in some cases, seem to flow from the rest of the petal. In the diagram, petal A does not flow from the rest of the petal, but in petal B, there is a continuous line. Be sure to hook at least an ELE into the edge of the petal to ensure the continuity. As the rollover is narrow, there is a special technique used to blend the values. You might look on it as your loops stumbling along the rollover. With a value #2, hook a loop, then one next to it, then drop down a row and hook a loop right below your second loop. Then, return to the initial row, and hook a loop or two, and then repeat, dropping down to hook a loop in the lower row. Stagger this a little so it doesn't form a regular pattern. With your value #1, hook beside the loops that are in place, remembering to hook up between the value #2 loops where there are gaps. If there is room for three values in the rollover, continue staggering the loops, dropping down a row in a random fashion.

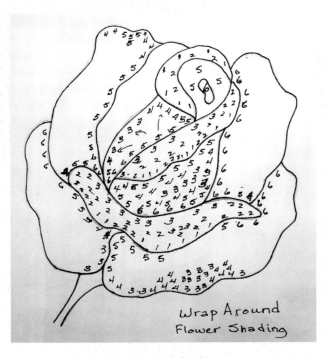

Wraparound shading.

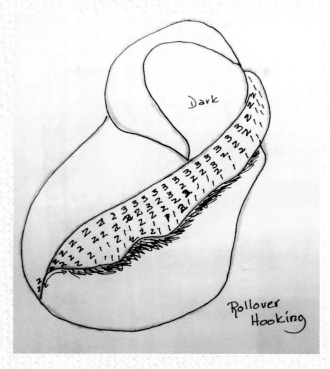

Rollover hooking.

Leaves

There are three basic types of leaves: a simple oval (morning glory) with or without a point; a lobed lea, with the lobes being pointed (maple leaf) or rounded (oak); and a strap leaf (daffodil). The major difference in the structure and thus the hooking of a leaf is that leaves tend to have either a single vein or a central vein with offshoots from that.

If there is a vein in the leaf, use a texture or a strip of the wool from one of your flowers to hook the vein. If it is long, you should start at the stem end with a dark value and lighten as you go up the leaf. Offshoots/branches of the vein use the same technique and may be lighter than the central vein. Most veins end before they get to the tip of the leaf. This applies to any shape of leaf.

Simple oval

Shading of the simple oval is done with mock shading (see glossary). This type of shading results in a pleasant roll to the leaf. Start to hook on one side of the central vein. For a small leaf, start with value #6 and hook along the vein from the stem end to a loop-and-end (LE) beyond the end of the vein. If the stem end of the leaf has a rounded area, start your value #6 a couple of loops before you get to the stem end of the vein. For a larger leaf, you will end the value #6 partway along the vein.

Next to the darkest value, hook in your #5 going along beside value #6 and past it a by couple of loops. Continue hooking in decreasing values until you have the lightest shade along the edge of the leaf. Depending on how wide your leaf is, you may need to add some more of the values #5, #4, or #3 in the centre of the leaf, but not extending it to the top or the base of the leaf.

   The other side of the leaf is done in reverse order of light and dark. Start with the value #1, the lightest shade, along the vein. If the vein is too long for one value, start the value #1 toward the tip of the leaf and change to a value #2 as you near the stem. Next to the value #1, hook in a value #2 and so on, till the value along the edge of the leaf is a value #6. Again, if the leaf is broad, you may need to add extra values #3, #4, and #5 to the central area of the leaf. Remember to follow the contours of the leaf.

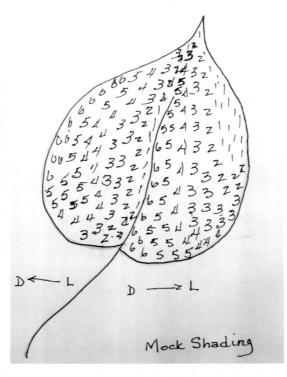

Mock shading.

THE GARRETT BLUENOSE PATTERNS

Lobed leaf

You will use fingering on the lobed leaf, although your "dark" lines from fingering the petals will be the veins. Start with value #6 and go up the vein and out partway along the first of the branches. Finish the branch with value #5, remembering to do a loop-and-end beyond the vein. As you move up the leaf, and as the vein gets lighter, adjust the shade you put next to the vein and branches. If you run into an area in which you have too much width between the loops on one branch and those on the next branch, take the last shade you worked with and add a short line in the middle, and then hook around it as you would around the branches. As with the petals, for a sharp pointed lobe, it is better to clip the wool at the top of the vein and then use a fresh strip of wool on the other side of the vein. With a rounded lobe, this may not be as necessary.

A lobed leaf.

Strap leaf

This is another occasion to use the mock shading technique. The variation here is due to the length of the leaf. Therefore, along the vein, you will need to change from value #6 to value #5 and perhaps to value #4. Keep that transition as you continue to hook from the darker values across to the lighter ones. However, you will need to stagger where you switch from one value to the next in order to avoid a marked line between the values.

Turnovers

Leaves of any shape, but especially strap leaves, tend to have turnovers. For strap leaves, the weight and length make them bend. As in the wraparound flower, the turnover creates a shadow. You will need to clearly delineate this shadow. Especially with the leaf, continue the outer (shadow-producing) edge of the turnover with at least an ELE or even an ELLE into the main part of the leaf in order for the turnover to appear to be part of the leaf.

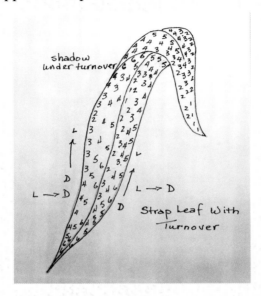

A strap leaf with turnover.

A Few Final Words

If in doubt, look at a photo of a flower or a leaf and assess where the darkest and lightest sections are and the transition between them. Look for the highlights; check how a turnover or rollover continues into the main part of the flower or leaf. If you can, look at a photo of the object in grey-scale (black and white). The shadows will really pop out. Take a breath and mimic what you see. Relax and enjoy bringing your garden to life.

References

Field, Jeanne. *Shading Flowers: The Complete Guide for Rug Hookers*. Pennsylvania: Stackpole Books, 1991.

Halliwell Green, Jane. *Rug in Bloom: Shading Flowers in Hooked Rugs*. Pennsylvania: Stackpole Books, 2012.

McGown, Pearl. "Notes," from a correspondence course in rug hooking, circa 1970.

Norman, Doris. "Selected diagrams for fingering and mock shading," circa 2003.

"A Rug Hooker's Garden," *Rug Hooking Magazine*, IV, Framework Series, 2000.

Finishing

Shirley Joyce

We have taken our time to choose our pattern, materials, and colours, and taken our time to hook our rug and make it just the way we want it. We step back and view our beautiful labour of love, and then comes the last of our work: the finishing. We have taken all this time to hook our rug; we should take the same pleasure in finishing it.

The following instructions are the basics taught today. There are variations you may have seen or heard, but if you know this method, then you're ready to finish your rug as a professional.

Supplies needed:

1. Darning needle or dull-ended needle.
2. Yarn of choice.
3. Ruler.
4. Sewing machine (or a friend with one).
5. Marker.
6. Rope or cording of choice.
7. Pins or T-pins.
8. Binding.
9. Thread to match binding.
10. Regular sewing needle.

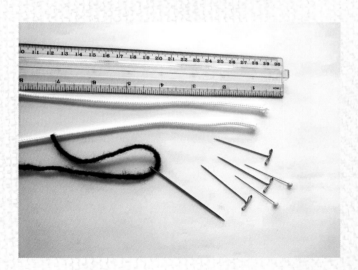

STEP 1. After pressing your rug (using the method described in "A Compilation of Tips and Tricks," page 106), lay it out on a flat surface. Using your ruler and marker, measure 1½ inches (3.8 centimetres) from the last hooked row of your rug. You have marked your sewing line. Using a sewing machine or serger, sew your marked line. If using a sewing machine, use a zigzag stitch and trim excess backing close to the stitching.

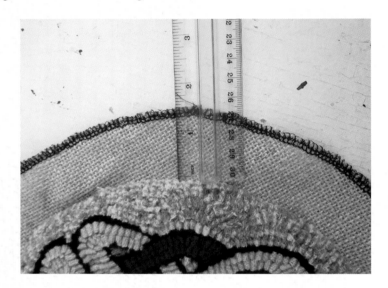

Cord/rope: Your cord should be no thicker than the height of your hooking. The average would be a ⅛-inch thickness—a little larger for a higher loop and thinner for a lower loop. Your cord should go all the way around your rug with a little extra (in case of the cord fraying). When buying the cord for your rug, please do not buy the yellow nylon cord. It is too thick and doesn't produce the best finish for your rug.

STEP 2. Place your cord under your linen up against your last hooked row and place a pin to hold it. Run your cord all the way around the rug, holding it in place with pins. When pinning at the corners, do not pull it tight. I tell people to relax a little so it isn't tight. Once you have your cord pinned in place, use Scotch tape to wrap the ends of the cord to prevent fraying. Time to whip!

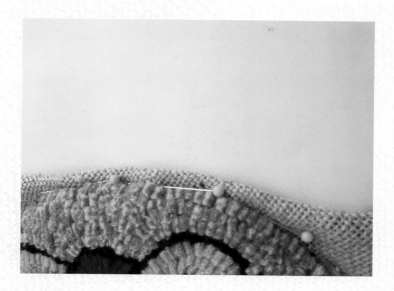

Yarn: The best thickness for whipping is 3-ply yarn. Most people use wool yarn to whip, but you can use any yarn you wish; just keep in mind where your rug will be placed once it's finished. If it's going on the floor, the best would be wool yarn. (For these instructions, I refer to wool yarn.)

STEP 3. Thread your darning needle or dull-ended needle with your wool yarn. You will be using one strand. I use my arms to measure the amount of yarn needed to thread the needle. Yes, my arms. Measure the yarn against your fully outstretched arms, and that is the length that you will use.

You can begin from the back or the front. Personally, I whip from the back to the front, so I will provide those instructions to you.

Taking your threaded needle, insert it from the back to the front between the chord and the last row of loops. Leave a 1-inch (2.5-cm) tail of wool to weave in later, or, using your free hand, hold it in place to whip over it at the beginning. Again, insert your needle from the back to the front (in the next hole), going right beside the previous stitch. Use your index finger to keep the yarn next to the last stitch. Do not skip any holes. Give just a slight tug on the wool so it isn't loose. The object of this is to cover the backing; you do not want any backing showing. Continue in this fashion. This is called "whipping." When you're close to running out of yarn, draw the remaining yarn to the back of your work and weave it into the back part of your whipping. Start again the same way as in the beginning, but this time, when you start, weave your needle of wool through the whipping at the back, then begin whipping from the back to the front as you have been doing, taking up where you left off.

Corners: Just because you hooked a square corner doesn't mean your corner will be whipped to look square; actually, it will be curved.

Just before you whip your corners, make sure they are ready. Take your T-pins or other pins out of the corner. To shape the corner, gather the backing in a curve over the cord so it is smooth, with no jagged edges. Make sure the cord is the same distance from your last hooked row as it has been all along. There may be a slight pleat on the back, but do your very best to smooth this out. A pleat will cause problems when whipping because it may poke through the wool you are whipping over it.

Once your corner is ready, start whipping. To make your curve, you will be whipping the same as you have been but with one difference: instead of going in each hole once, you will be going in each hole two to three times to make sure the linen is not showing. You really need to guide the wool and go slowly.

You have now almost finished whipping. You can cross over the ends of the cord, but this will make a lump. Instead, butt the ends of the cord together and whip over them, being careful not to make a gully where the cords meet. Your whipping is finished when your ends meet the beginning.

THE GARRETT BLUENOSE PATTERNS

STEP 4. Now it is time to bind the back of your rug, the last step to enjoying a finished rug. Your binding should be washed before you use it. Once washed, it is easier to use and will not bleed.

On the back of your rug, pin the binding along the bottom edge of the whipping. When you come to the corners, they need to be mitred. When the ends come together, lay one end over the other and fold under. You don't want any raw edges showing.

Sew, starting at the top of the binding using a regular needle and thread that matches the colour of the binding. Once the top is finished, move to the bottom. This is trickier. You must remember not to stitch on a hooked loop for it will pull that loop out. If your stitch has to go through a hooked loop, then make sure you go through it and grab a part of the backing; this way if the thread pulls, it will tug at the backing and not your hooked loop. When you come to the corners, stitch the mitred corner and continue sewing until you come to the end.

The object is to stitch grabbing the backing. If all else fails, and you have no other choice, then follow these instructions: put your needle in between your hooked loops, run it under the loop, and grab the backing; skip it along and bring it back up. This way you're not going right into the hooked loop but instead grabbing the backing under it.

You will be excited when it comes to the binding, knowing this is the end, but please take your time. After all the work you have put into the beautiful rug, the last thing you want is ugly-looking stitches on your binding. It is just as important that the stitching looks as good as your hooking.

DONE! You have now finished your beautiful rug. Enjoy.

In Summary

~~~ ⚬⚬ ~~~

Ruth Downing

The members of the Teachers Branch are very proud to have played a part in resurrecting and preserving the Bluenose patterns. These patterns are now in the public domain. Copyright no longer applies. However, the Teachers Branch does own the acetate stencils.

The acetate images are accessible to all members of the Rug Hooking Guild of Nova Scotia as a PDF on the Guild's website (rhgns.com). Numbered, sized, and categorized by subject the images are excellent in clarity, available to view in the gallery, and may be downloaded for enlargement to print at a nominal cost.

With great appreciation, the Teachers Branch would like to acknowledge the following people. Their enthusiastic support has given us purpose, and with their generosity this historic project has moved forward to completion:

- Eldon MacDonald—you believe in the Teachers Branch organization and the work we do. You knew we could successfully care for the stencils and complete this project for your wife, Linda. Thank you for this incredible gift!
- Anne Sutherland—thank you for the lovely glimpse into the world of your great-grandfather, John Garrett, and family. Without your timeless photographs, their faces and surroundings would remain in our imaginations. Now we have a clearer picture of who they were.
- Suzanne Conrod—thank you for your kind generosity and permission to take so many photographs of the wonderful Garrett art and history on-site at the Hooked Rug Museum of North America. The treasure trove of pencil sketches and ink drawings has magically taken us into the past.
- Our gratitude is extended to the many rug hookers who took the time to photograph their beautiful rugs and patterns for submission. We so appreciate all the creativity and talent displayed in these pages.

In closing, it is our hope that all who read this book will be inspired to hook a Bluenose rug and encourage others to do the same.

Glossary of Terms

Caroline M. Simpson

antigodlin   A technique used to fill an area without showing direction, so that no two loops line up in a row. Each time you pull up a loop, remove your hook and change the direction in which the point of the hook faces, then pull up another loop, and so on. It helps the viewer see the shape and colour of an object without being pointed in any particular direction. Often used to fill in skies.

backing   The cloth through which the loops are hooked. The most common types of backing are burlap (also called jute or hessian), linen, monks cloth, and rug warp. Depending on the tightness of the weave, the backing may be more suited to a primitive style or a fine cut.

blending   Mixing one or more colours into another to create a soft transition with no harshly defined border.

Bluenose   The name of the company founded by the Garrett family of New Glasgow, NS, in tribute to the famous Nova Scotian *Bluenose* racing and fishing schooner.

burlap   A woven fabric, made from the skin of the jute plant or sisal fibres, used as a backing for rug hooking. Also called hessian or jute. In the past, thrifty crafters would repurpose flour and seed bags made of burlap to use as the backing for their mats.

cording   Cotton cord or rope used for finishing a rug. The cord is placed close to the outside edge of the hooking on the back of the mat. The unhooked border of backing is folded over the cord and tacked in place and then the backing-covered cord is whip-stitched with wool yarn or encased in strips of felted wool.

crossover   A strip of wool that is carried over a previous row of hooking to avoid having to clip it and bring up a new end. This practice is frowned upon in traditional rug hooking as it causes a bump on the back and is more likely to experience wear and tear when the mat is used on the floor; it also looks messy on the back side. However, in today's hooking, crossovers are acceptable in hooked wall hangings and framed pictures.

cut	The size of the strip of wool used. Cuts are measured by ⅟₃₂-inch, and the most common cuts are numbers 2 to 10, which correspond, respectively, to ⅟₁₆-inch (number 2) to ¼-inch (number 8) to ½-inch (number 10).
cutter	A small, portable machine used to cut strips of wool to a uniform size. Common types of cutters available today are Fraser, Bliss, Rigby, Beeline Townsend, HoneyDoo, and Bolivar. Some types (Beeline Townsend, HoneyDoo, and Bolivar) offer a "kit-maker" cartridge that will cut more strips at a single pass, and some brands (e.g., Bliss, HoneyDoo) also have an electric option for those who are cutting large quantities of strips.
cutter cartridge	Interchangeable accessories to Beeline Townsend, HoneyDoo, and Bolivar cutters that change the cut of the machine to the various standard sizes (i.e., cuts numbers 2 to 10)
cutter wheel	Interchangeable accessories to Fraser, Bliss, and Rigby cutters that change the cut of the machine to the various standard sizes (i.e., cuts numbers 2 to 10).
directional hooking	A method where the hooked loops all follow the same direction. It's often used to outline a shape or to fill inside a shape, but it may simply be used to hook straight across a mat to form the background. It's particularly useful to draw the eye from one area of design to another and can create a sense of motion.
ditch	The space between two parallel threads in the weave of a backing material. You can mark the straight grain of the fabric by running a pencil or pen along the "ditch" and ensure that your pattern is drawn accurately so the finished rug won't appear warped.
door peeper	The small reducing glass device used for door peepholes; it can be used to view your work as if at a distance, helping you see whether the perspective is off, or if values contrast or blend. Available at most hardware stores.
embellishment	Items such as sea glass, beads, buttons, wire, or "fantasy" yarns used to add dimension and interest to a hooked piece.
end-loop-end	The smallest amount of hooking that can be done on a piece that will remain stable. One end of a strip is brought up through a hole in the backing, then a loop is hooked through the next hole and the strip is then pulled to the top through the next hole after that and clipped.
feathering	Blending different values of a swatch from dark to light or light to dark to avoid a sharp or harsh delineation. The transition from one value to another is achieved by randomly staggering one to two loops of the next value into the finishing edge of the previous value. Similar to "fingering."

fine shading	Style of hooking using numbers 6- or 8-value swatches and using techniques such as feathering, fingering, and mock shading to achieve a realistic interpretation of an object, such as a flower or fruit.
fingering	Blending different values of a swatch in between other values from dark to light or light to dark—to avoid a sharp or harsh delineation—following a pattern like that formed when the fingers of two hands mesh together Similar to "feathering."
finishing	Techniques used to finish the edge of a hooked piece, such as cording, whipping, and binding; folding under and hemming; encasing with felted wool strips; backing with felted wool cut to measure; stapling over stretcher bars or artist's canvas; or framing.
foundation	The cloth through which loops are hooked; also called "backing."
frame	The device used to stretch and hold the backing material taut. Frames can be mounted on a stand or used on a table or on your lap. Some frames have wire "gripper" strips to catch the fabric and hold it in place, whereas others require the fabric to be tacked or sewn in place. Common brands or types of frames include Pilgrim, Snapdragon, and Cheticamp.
Garrett	Family name of the Nova Scotian father and sons who popularized and standardized rug hooking patterns and tools in the late nineteenth century. The firm continued in business for eighty years.
geometric	Mat design that features motifs predominantly based on geometric forms. Many are modified versions of quilt patterns. Depending on the colour planning, some may appear three dimensional, e.g. the classic "tumbling blocks" pattern.
gradation	A gradual transition from one colour to another or the shift in values of a colour (or colours) from dark to light or vice versa.
grain	The direction of threads in a fabric. The lengthwise grain is the direction that the warp runs, parallel to the selvage edge; the crosswise grain follows the direction of the weft. The lengthwise grain is stronger and more stable.
gripper strip	Strips of tempered steel wire teeth that are attached to a hooking or punching frame to hold backing fabric in place and tightly stretched. They are very durable but, if necessary, replacement strips can be purchased either pre-cut to fit your frame or as a continuous roll that you can cut to measure.
hessian cloth	Another name for burlap.

higglety-pigglety   The technique of randomly hooking your wool strips in a meandering fashion (rather than straight back and forth) to fill in a background or large area. See also "antigodlin." Opposite of directional hooking.

holiday   Bare spot in the hooking that needs to be filled in. Before finishing your mat, check the back for holidays, mark them with toothpicks or T-pins, turn the mat over, and fill in the marked spots.

hue   Hue is the name of the colour, referring to dominant colour family, i.e., the primary and secondary colours yellow, orange, red, violet, blue, and green. Tertiary colours (e.g., red-violet) are also considered hues.

jump   Carrying a strip (or yarn) over the back of already hooked loops (also called "skip"); not recommended practice as it weakens the rug, but is sometimes acceptable in wall hangings.

jute   Another name for burlap.

linen   Material used for the foundation or backing of the mat. Linen comes in different weaves, with coarser weaves used for primitive designs/wide cuts, and fine weaves used for fine cuts. Linen also comes in "hairy" and "hairless" varieties.

loop   The shape formed by a strip of wool that is pulled up through a hole in the weave of the backing cloth.

mock shading   A technique used for giving a three-dimensional look to an object by using value swatches in sequential order to simulate the shadowing that would appear when light hits an object. Often used when hooking "strap" leaves such as those found on irises or tulips. The shape of the leaf is hooked along its length in, for example, the darkest value of the swatch, then the next-darkest value is hooked alongside the first line, and so on, until the lightest value is reached at the centre of the leaf. Then the sequence is repeated on the other side of the leaf from the centre out to the edge.

monks cloth   A type of backing or foundation cloth that has a very even regular weave and is made of cotton. It has more stretch than linen and also has a regular 1-inch (2.5-cm) grid marked in the weave that some find very useful when hooking. Very suitable for rug punching.

mordant   A setting agent used to fix the dye in cloth or yarn. Common mordants used with wool are vinegar, citric acid, Glauber's salt.

packing   Hooking rows of loops too close together; also, hooking into every hole in the row of the backing. Places strain on the backing material, and can prevent the mat from lying flat, even after steaming/pressing.

padula	An imaginary flower, often seen in primitive designs.
pictorial	A mat that depicts a scene or picture.
primitive	Rug designs in the folk-art tradition, these are simple designs that do not necessarily reflect correct proportions. There is usually little or no attempt to shade motifs.
punching	Pushing yarn with a punch hook, through a backing, creating a rug with uniform loops in a highly textured pattern; also, a primitive method of settling disputes.
red dot	A nonwoven dot graph material made of Pellon®. It features an accurate 1-inch (2.5-cm) graph, used for scaling up, duplicating, or altering patterns.
reverse hooking	A creative stitch formed by pulling loops through the reverse side of your foundation, creating a smooth fill of flat strips on the right side.
rollover	Area in which the petal or leaf turns back on itself showing its underside (also see "turnover")
rug warp	Type of backing cloth; a plain weave, cotton fabric that is a little heavier than linen and monk's cloth and is less stretchy.
shading	Techniques using swatches of different values of a colour to imitate the shadows and highlights on an object.
skip	A) A blank spot on the right side where the backing cloth shows through the hooking; B) An area where one strip has been crossed over the back of another row of hooking, creating a bump that will be subject to greater wear and tear (also see "jump").
staggering	A) A special blending technique used along narrow rollovers when fine shading; B) A way to avoid having an unsightly "ditch" on your rug by staggering where you pull up and clip the ends of strips.
strip	An evenly cut, narrow length of felted wool fabric that is used to create a pile by pulling it up in loops through the holes in the backing.
swatch	A set of colour values (usually 6 or 8) forming a gradient from dark to light of felted wool. Common sizes for swatches are 3 x 12 inches (7.5 x 30.5 cm) or 4 x 18 inches (10 x 46 cm), but many other sizes are used too. Can also refer to a single strip of felted wool.
tail	The end of a strip that is pulled up through the backing cloth. Each strip hooked will have two tails.

texture	Woven fabric that has a design or special weave, such as jacquard, plaid, or nubbly wool. Use of textures can add interest and depth to your design. They are very useful in creating realistic animal fur/skin, and are commonly used in primitives.
turnover	An area where a petal or leaf is bent over on itself so that both the top and underside are visible (also see "rollover").
value	The lightness or darkness of a colour.
weave	The manner in which the warp and filling threads (weft) interlace with each other. For rug hooking, an evenly spaced weave is preferred for the backing cloth. For the wool strips, a flannel weave that has been lightly felted is the easiest to work with.
wetting agent	Added to the water when presoaking fabric before dyeing, it helps the fabric open up its fibres to accept the dye. Synthrapol is a commercial wetting agent, but a drop or two of common dishwashing detergent does the job too.
whipping	The process of covering up the folded-over backing on the edge of the mat by darning yarn over it all the way around the edge using an overcast stitch. It helps protect, strengthen, and decorate the edge.

642 Original ink drawing, 3 x 4 inches,
courtesy of HRMNA.

THE GARRETT BLUENOSE PATTERNS

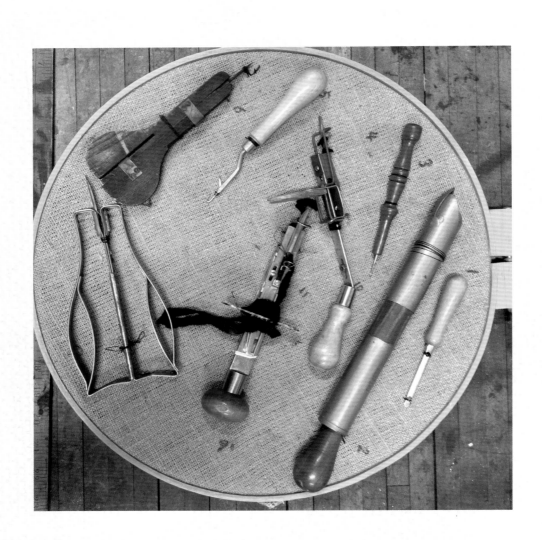